Godwinks for Moms

Godwinks for Moms

TRUE STORIES

SQuire Rushnell
and Louise DuArt

LARGE PRINT PRESS
A part of Gale, a Cengage Company

GALE
A Cengage Company

GALE
A Cengage Company

Large Print Press, a part of Gale, a Cengage Company.

The text of this Large Print edition is unabridged.
Other aspects of the book may vary from the original edition.
Set in 16 pt. Plantin.

**LIBRARY OF CONGRESS CIP DATA ON FILE.
CATALOGUING IN PUBLICATION FOR THIS BOOK
IS AVAILABLE FROM THE LIBRARY OF CONGRESS.**

ISBN-13: 978-1-4205-2758-2 (paperback alk. paper)

Published in 2025 by arrangement with Howard Books, an Imprint of Simon & Schuster, LLC.

Printed in Mexico
1 2 3 4 5 6 7 29 28 27 26 25

CONTENTS

10. "MAMA BEAR" MOMS

11. GRIEVING MOMS FIND HOPE

INTRODUCTION

Fitting perfectly . . . like Mom's hand in God's glove . . . these three words go together:

Mother
Universally synonymous with hugs, comfort, and safety.

Mom
An abbreviation of Mother . . . easier for kids to yell: "Hey, Mom!"

Godwinks
A relatively new word in our language for signs of hope from divine origin.

This book captures real stories of real moms and their astonishing Godwink experiences.

Many of the stories will touch you so deeply and directly that you'll think we're telling *your* story about *you* as a mom. Or about *your* mom.

For instance, you'll read about a mother who sends her daughter off to tackle the world. Into the girl's hand she slips a famous poem of inspiration called "Footprints in the Sand," by author unknown. "Whenever you feel alone, this poem will remind you that you're *never* alone," said the mother. Yet, as you journey with the young woman, Godwinks astonishingly lead you to the poem's author . . . who wrote it at age fourteen.

You'll feel the heartache of a young mother who tragically loses a succession of babies to miscarriages. But you'll quickly fall in love with her constant companion . . . a comical golden retriever named Bullet . . . a true-life hero who leads the way to the happiest Godwink outcome you could possibly imagine.

A teen mother weeps over her newborn as she reluctantly releases him to adoption, pledging to pray for him every day. But the way in which Godwinks led that child back to her, years later, is both heartwarming and astonishing.

■ ■ ■ ■

A mother and daughter, both larger-than-life personalities, each give birth to a special-needs child. They have no idea that God's plan is for them to form a team of dedicated teachers in the creation of one of the world's most respected and joyful communities for special-needs adults.

If you wish to connect with your own memories *as* a mom . . . or recollections about *your* mom . . . we invite you to read on!

And if something you read fosters an urge to share a story of your own, we'd love to hear it:

www.Stories@Godwinks.com

1
When Moms Pray — Godwinks Happen

1A
Brittany I — How Many Blessings for Mommy?

From the age of seven, Brittany embraced her childhood dream to strive for the most cherished career destination of all: being a mom!

As a mini-mommy, she dedicated hours to dressing up her baby dolls for school, preparing their make-believe meals, and teaching them right from wrong.

"Don't cry, Emily . . . let Mommy kiss your hurt. Andy didn't mean to push you — did you, Andy."

When her sister Kelley came along — three years younger — they played Barbies and babies together. Sister Ally was eight years younger, so when Ally was old enough, Brittany was in her teens playing dolls with her.

Finally, when young Matthew arrived, twelve years between them, people said Brittany was like a real-life "little mom" to him. A natural caregiver, always offering a shoulder to lean on.

In fact, her mom and dad both worked, so the children often stayed with their grandparents. "But while we were there," admits Brittany, "I always looked after my siblings."

When Brittany went off to college, she selected a field of study closest to preparing her for motherhood: a teaching and coaching education. It didn't hurt that by that time she excelled at basketball.

Through her twenties, Brittany's dream to be a mother never left her mind, notwithstanding the prerequisite — marriage.

After graduation, she began teaching seventh-grade math and coaching girls' basketball at Central Cambria High School in Ebensburg, Pennsylvania, east of Pittsburgh.

One of Brittany's players was the sister of a handsome young athlete and schoolteacher, Josh Bracken, who occasionally — actually, more and more occasionally — came by to watch his sister Jackie play. From Josh's point of view, there was definitely something alluring about his sister's funny, happy-go-lucky, and really pretty basketball coach, Brittany. Moreover, they had something in common — Josh was a coach himself. Baseball.

Brittany and Josh's relationship began to

develop when they hung out together, becoming very good friends — that is, until a kiss seemed to stop the world and put everything onto a more serious path. They dated and got to know each other for three years before Josh started planning how he would propose.

Josh and his guy friends had a hunting camp located in the woodlands of northern Pennsylvania, a few hours from home. He knew that in late spring the state flower, pink-and-white mountain laurel, would bloom all along the forest trails, creating a magical environment. That's where he asked Brittany to marry him. It was sweet and romantic. A year later they stood by each other's side and became husband and wife. Brittany was thirty-three and ready to fulfill her life's quest — to be a mom! Within weeks she was expecting!

Then, at around seven weeks' pregnant, the worst of news: Brittany miscarried.

The sense of loss seemed unbearable. "I was devastated and heartbroken," she said.

As soon as possible, the young couple tried again. And again.

Brittany fretted to her mother, Stephanie, "Everyone around me is having successful pregnancies. Yet month after month, I'm still not pregnant!"

She prayed and prayed. Nothing happened.

Still grieving the loss of her first child, she began to question why God was not responding. She became disheartened.

"That's when I picked up a book, *Godwink Stories: A Devotional.* I found hope in the Godwink stories of others. I felt encouraged. If good things could happen to those people, they could happen to me too. I began praying for a Godwink to assure me that we were going to have a baby."

But when a positive pregnancy test continued to elude her, Brittany lamented to her mother that "God doesn't answer me."

Stephanie, a surgical nurse, had always taught her children the power of prayer. Moreover, better than anyone, she knew that God had placed a deep desire for motherhood into Brittany's heart at a very early age.

Feeling helpless, Stephanie followed her own counsel, increasing her own prayers for her sweet daughter. "Please, God, let Brittany experience the joy of pregnancy."

A few days later, Stephanie was traveling to California to help Matthew, her youngest, pack up things in his dorm, getting them in storage for summer break at Pepperdine

University.

Well experienced at this task, with several kids, Stephanie had a routine. Take all of the linens and Matt's clothing to a laundromat, then box and label them so they'll be fresh in the fall.

An older gentleman came into the laundromat. He had a kindly look about him. He smiled at Stephanie, commented on her cross necklace, and asked if she had grandchildren.

Stephanie struck up a conversation with the gentleman, sharing that only one of her four children was married. She added that Brittany and her husband had experienced the tragedy of miscarriage and were frustrated that they'd been unable to succeed since.

The man looked at Stephanie, his eyes twinkling as he spoke.

"You tell her to be kind . . . to pray . . . have faith . . . and she will be blessed double!"

He held her gaze. "Do you know what I mean?"

Stephanie answered tentatively, "Twins?"

He nodded. "Tell her that Herb said she'll be twice blessed!"

Stephanie couldn't wait to phone Brittany. Was this the Godwink she was praying for?

Brittany took her mother's encounter with the man named Herb as a sign.

"I kept trying, kept the faith," said Brittany, "and six months later I finally got my positive pregnancy test!"

Brittany and Josh scheduled an early ultrasound because of her prior loss.

The weekend before their appointment, Josh was up at his hunting camp and encountered a man who ran the Moose Club. He talked about his granddaughter and was selling raffle tickets to her event. Josh bought one, subsequently discovering that the man's name, ironically, was Herb.

On their way to the ultrasound a couple of days later, Brittany wondered, *Is there any heavenly connection between the two Herbs?*

They felt an inner excitement as the ultrasound tech performed the procedures . . . and a spike of curiosity when the tech smiled, turned the screen to them, and said, "What do you see?"

As clear as day, the ultrasound photography showed two sacs! And underneath, typed on the screen, was: "Baby A . . . Baby B . . . Twins!"

"I felt exuberance! A peace came over me that I knew was God's presence," said Brittany. "I got my Godwinks!"

POSTSCRIPT

Three months before this book was published, Brittany and Josh learned the genders of the babies — twin boys!

However, because the twins will be born a month after publication, photos can be seen at www.godwinks.com for one year.

REFLECTIONS

Brittany's desire for motherhood was spirited and resolute.

Yet every month that she failed to conceive, she felt a little more disheartened, questioning if there was something wrong with her or wondering if God simply had not heard her pleas.

Hannah and Sarah from the Bible experienced similar frustration. But in the end, God answered each of their prayers as well as Brittany's.

The kind words of the stranger named Herb — spoken with absolute authority — ignited a beacon of hope within Brittany, to stay the course, to keep on praying and to keep the faith.

She did. And the ultrasound confirmed exactly what Herb had said: She would have double blessings! Twins.

During times when we don't see God working, we need to be persistent in our prayers but patient in our faith. He does some of His best work in the waiting.

> Rejoicing in hope, patient in tribulation, continuing steadfastly in prayer.
>
> — ROMANS 12:12 (NKJV)

1B
Diane's Country Church Nudge

Diane Baum, a warmhearted and compassionate woman whose generosity of spirit knows no bounds, had agreed to care for the animals of a friend who went out of town for the weekend.

Dogs. Cats. Goats. Chickens. They all needed to be fed.

Glancing at the kitchen clock and seeing it was 5:30 p.m., Diane grabbed her car keys and asked her husband, Rob, if he wanted to join her. An animal lover, Rob jumped at the chance to go to the farm and hang out with all the little critters.

It was mid-September in central Minnesota, where the sun goes down just after 7 p.m., taking with it the warmth of the day.

As Diane and Rob drove down the little country road toward the farm it was nearly six o'clock and there was a chill in the air.

As they passed a tiny, white, old-fashioned-looking church, Diane noticed a familiar car in the parking lot.

"Oh, there's Kathryn," she said. "She must be there with Bobby."

Diane's good friend Kathryn had a severely autistic son whom she would often take to the little playground at the back of the church to settle him down from his feelings of anxiety.

The church sat alone on the prairie, surrounded by acres of cornfields. Quiet and secluded, it was a peaceful escape from the noise and chaos of other children in the playgrounds at schools and parks.

It was the perfect place to let Bobby swing and run around.

Diane and Rob continued on their way.

They stayed at the farm, tending the animals for forty-five minutes before heading back home.

As they passed the church again, Diane said, "Oh, look. Kathryn's still there."

At the church, Kathryn was beside herself with worry.

She had taken her son to the playground to relax after a long day at school.

Seven years old and severely autistic, Bobby was a ball of energy. And if Kathryn didn't come up with creative ways to burn off some of that energy, Bobby could potentially harm himself, and others, or wreck the house.

So Kathryn often brought him to the isolated church playground to swing, climb, and play, while she sat on a bench, watching him and reading her Bible or praying.

That was her plan that day.

However, as they disembarked from Kathryn's truck, Bobby bounced out of the back seat and slammed the door shut. On the way, he must have struck the lock button with his elbow.

Kathryn's vehicle was now locked, with her purse, car keys, cell phone, and Bobby's shoes still inside.

And it was growing cold.

The church was five miles from Diane's house, and another mile from Kathryn's, too far for Bobby to walk barefoot to either one. In his severely anxious state, they would likely not have made it.

When Kathryn and Bobby first arrived, someone was at the church running a quick errand and had let them inside to use the phone.

Calls to both Kathryn's husband and mother went to voicemail. But Kathryn, confident that one of them would pick up her message and come to her aid, told the church worker not to worry, to lock up, and sent him on his way.

Oh, how she now wished she hadn't done that!

It had been quite a while since she'd made her calls, and neither Kathryn's husband nor mother had arrived. She watched the sun descending quickly enough to be scary.

Kathryn and Bobby were officially stranded.

So, Kathryn began praying. She didn't know what else to do.

"Lord, help us," she pleaded as the sun moved closer to the horizon and the temperature dropped. "Please, send someone to help us!"

As time ticked on, panic built up within Kathryn, as she fought to shield her feelings from Bobby so as not to set him off.

On their way home from the farm, Diane and Rob had just passed the church. Diane drove another hundred yards or so, then slammed on the brakes.

"We need to go back," Diane announced. "We need to check on things."

"At the farm?" Rob asked.

"No. We need to check on Kathryn. Something's wrong."

As clearly as if someone had pasted a sign

on her windshield, Diane knew all was not right.

She sensed a strong voice in her head, with firm instructions.

You need to go back, it urged. *Now.*

So Diane did a U-turn on the narrow country road.

And back they drove.

It felt as though they'd been at the church for hours, when a car finally turned in to the parking lot.

Kathryn rapidly drew in a breath of surprise . . . and relief! In the dim light that was left of the day, she recognized Diane and Rob's car!

"How are you doing?" asked Diane. "What's going on?"

Kathryn's face contorted, uncontrollable tears poured from her eyes, and she ran to hug her friend.

It took a few moments for Kathryn to compose herself and to provide Diane and Rob with an explanation.

Now everything made sense to Diane.

If she hadn't noticed Kathryn's car at the church in the first place, or if she hadn't slammed on the brakes and turned around when it was still there, she would have missed Kathryn and Bobby completely.

They would have been stuck in the dark and cold, and left to the dangers of the night.

But God had heard Kathryn's prayers, even before she prayed them, and arranged to send the cavalry . . . Diane and Rob.

Diane told Kathryn and Bobby to hop into her SUV; she and Rob would take them home.

"But my keys are in the truck," said Kathryn. "I won't have a way to get into my house and my extra key to the truck."

"I do," Diane exclaimed, lifting her key chain to show Kathryn a big brass house key.

Kathryn had given Diane the key to her home years ago when her family went on vacation, but until that moment, everyone had forgotten.

So Diane and Rob drove Kathryn and Bobby home, got them inside, and made plans for Kathryn to drive back the next day with her husband to pick up her car.

"How did you know?" asked Rob over and over, incredulously. "How did you know Kathryn needed help?"

From time to time, years later, Rob would still shake his head and say, "I just don't understand how you knew. But thank God you did!"

Diane still passes that little church on her

way into town.

Every time, she smiles and says, "Thank you, God!"

It was a Godwink for the ages!

Reflections

When Kathryn prayed, God went to work by sending Diane a nudge to turn back and check on her friend.

As a child of God, your spirit is like a receiver connected to a heavenly antenna. He is sending signals all the time. Our job is to keep our receiver tuned to His channel.

Sometimes God's voice comes as a whisper. In the moment, you may not fully comprehend what's happening . . . but deep within your heart, you just know, He's guiding you. Diane acted on the signal in her spirit, resulting in an incredible Godwink.

God is constantly speaking to us and giving us His direction.

Let's always ask: Is my receiver turned on? Tuned in to God?

He broadcasts 24/7.

The gatekeeper opens the gate for him,
and the sheep listen to his voice.
He calls his own sheep by name and
leads them out.

— John 10:3–4 (NIV)

1C
Darla and Danella — Young Mother's Prayer

What should have been the most joyful day for seventeen-year-old Darla Svenby was instead one of the most heartbreaking days of her life.

After a scary night of labor, Darla learned the baby was breech and that a cesarean section was required.

Then the unmarried teenager gave birth to a healthy baby boy!

Yet joy eluded her. The adoptive parents were eager to take her baby home, leaving Darla with a wrenching emptiness in her heart . . . wondering if she would ever see her child . . . let alone cuddle him.

"Please let me hold my baby," she pleaded, her eyes filling with tears. "I need to tell him goodbye."

Her nurse, Danella Walters, was a woman of faith with a heart of gold. She had chosen a nursing career to help people at their most vulnerable moments. Now she was looking into the eyes of a young mother whose pain was breaking her heart.

She knew the policy at St. Margaret's Hospital in Montgomery, Alabama — it wasn't permitted for the birth mother to bond with the adopted baby. Danella wrestled with that.

Darla's mother came into the room and saw her daughter crying. Thinking she could comfort her, Mrs. Svenby told Darla she had just returned from the nursery.

Darla's sobs evolved to hysteria!

Gently, her mother held her, wiped away the tears, and told her how she'd held the baby.

"He's perfect."

Those last words were the ones that calmed Darla.

She looked up at her mother's sweet face.

"He is? He's perfect?"

Mrs. Svenby nodded and smiled. "I held him . . . prayed for him . . . and promised our Lord that we would pray for him every day for the rest of our lives."

"We will, Mama."

That seemed to bring Darla some peace. But as soon as her mother left to get the baby an outfit to wear home . . . saying she wanted her grandchild to wear something that came from her . . . Darla was once more overcome with agonizing loss.

Nurse Danella brought in the birth certificate for Darla to fill out and sign, only to discover that the new mother was again spinning out of control with emotion.

Eventually Darla calmed down long enough to do the paperwork and give her baby a name to be placed on the birth certificate, even though she assumed the adoptive parents would choose a different name for him.

As Danella left the room with the paperwork, she noticed there was a momentary staff shortage due to the shift change. Surreptitiously, she reappeared moments later . . . carrying a bundle in a blanket . . . Darla's newborn son!

The surprise took Darla's breath away! She began to tremble . . . feeling a surge of joy and gratitude!

Danella gently placed the baby into Darla's arms and watched the loving scene unfolding before her. She felt admiration for the sacrifice this young mother was making for her baby.

The young mother studied her little boy, smelling of baby powder, telling him how much she loved him. She whispered that giving him up was not her choice, but she knew it was best for him.

Tears ran down her cheeks and onto his face as she kissed him all over his little head, repeating, "I'll love you and pray for you every single day. I promise."

When it was time for Darla to leave the hospital a day or two later, her boyfriend, Randy Allgood, arrived with Darla's parents.

As Danella watched them go, she couldn't help but notice the love and kindness they showed for each other, even during such a difficult time. Danella knew she would never forget them.

The seasons changed. The years passed. And in the blink of an eye, eighteen years had gone by.

By now Darla and Randy had married, the air force had moved them to Alaska, and they had four sons.

But Darla never forgot her pledge to pray daily for her firstborn.

Nurse Danella now had a daughter named Amanda, who was in a new relationship with a young man named Chad. Amanda brought him home for dinner to meet her family.

Danella liked Amanda's new boyfriend, but she sensed something of a chip on his shoulder. She couldn't articulate what it was exactly.

Then, after Amanda and Chad had been dating awhile, Danella asked him about his father and mother.

Chad was quick to reply that he didn't know his parents. Not his birth parents at least.

"All I know is that my birth mom gave me away the night I was born."

Danella's hackles began to rise.

"They gave me up for adoption at Jackson Hospital," he said, with a tinge of bitterness.

As soon as Danella heard that, she knew that was the chip she'd sensed.

Rising to the defense of birth mothers, Danella told Chad, "Young mothers don't just 'give up' their babies without tremendous distress. Many are tormented for years, not knowing what happened to their baby."

She explained that though she was now retired, she had been a nurse for years at St. Margaret's. She'd seen young women who were tormented as they placed their babies into adoption, particularly when they were conflicted, knowing they weren't prepared to be parents themselves.

"I remember one teenage mom who suffered so much grief and anguish that I broke the rules to let her hold her baby! I practically crawled onto the bed to comfort her as I watched that sweet mother cover her newborn's little face with tears and kisses."

She looked at Chad seriously. "You'll be eaten up inside . . . unless you find a way to forgive your parents."

She held her stare . . .

"How old are you, Chad?"

"Eighteen."

She tilted her head, ever so slightly . . . as if she was thinking about something.

"You were born in Jackson Hospital?"

He nodded.

Eventually, Amanda married Chad, and soon they were expecting a child of their own.

Danella had quietly suggested that, at age twenty-one, Chad would have access to his birth records. And once Chad realized he was going to be a father, he and Amanda promptly filed the papers.

As Chad sat at Danella's kitchen table, with Amanda and his mother-in-law, he carefully opened the yellow envelope. His hand pulled out the birth records, and his eyes fell upon the birth date that matched his own.

He read his birth mother's name aloud, saying it with great respect.

"Darla Svenby."

Danella's eyes instantly widened.

"It says I was born at St. Margaret's Hospital in Montgomery! Not Jackson?"

Danella knew what he'd read. And even though she couldn't remember the name that the young mother, Darla, had written on her baby's birth certificate eighteen years before, she'd felt all along that Chad could have been that very infant . . . from the day Amanda brought her new boyfriend home.

Slowly Danella's head moved side to side as she held Chad in her gaze. "Not Jackson . . . you were born at St. Margaret's."

They stared at each other for a long moment.

"I held you," continued Danella tenderly. "And your mother loved you with the most unselfish love. Nobody loved you more than she did. Bathing you in kisses. Now . . . go and find her."

Chad lifted his glistening eyes and nodded at his mother-in-law.

Svenby was an unusual last name, so Chad and Amanda were lucky. Though they'd struck out with the obvious searches, in the courthouse and online, a recent obituary came up for Darla's mother, Dolores Irene Svenby. It was just the lead he needed.

It led them to an Allgood family near an air force base in Alaska.

Randy Allgood surprised his wife, Darla, at her pottery shop and suggested they go out to lunch.

"Our son called," he finally said when they were seated at the restaurant.

"Yes? And what did Brandon, Adam, Casey, or Dillon need?" asked Darla jokingly.

"No," said Randy quietly. "Our other son . . . Chad."

Darla was stunned . . . speechless. It was the day she and her mother had prayed for, over and over again. The day when her first son would find his way back to her. And . . . thank you, Lord . . . his name was still Chad!

Her lip quivered. Tears formed instantly, pouring down her cheeks.

That evening Chad called, as had been arranged earlier with Randy. He and Darla talked for hours.

When their other sons discovered they had a big brother, they were ecstatic.

Finally, the day came for them to all meet. Chad and Amanda flew up to Alaska and the family waited at the airport to welcome them.

"What if he doesn't like me?" fretted Darla.

"Impossible," answered Randy, giving her hand a squeeze.

When the plane landed, Darla and Chad approached each other with their hearts in their throats. Once again they embraced — after all those years — and he laid his head on her shoulder just as he did the first time.

The emptiness in Darla's heart vanished. Instantly it was filled with love. And any lingering bitterness in Chad's heart evaporated.

When Darla and Randy learned that Amanda's mother was Danella — Darla's kind nurse from long ago, who had broken the rules by surreptitiously bringing Darla's son to her, to cover him in kisses — there was no doubt. It was God winking in direct response to hundreds of daily prayers by Darla and her dear mother in heaven!

POSTSCRIPT

In the weeks that followed, Darla went through her recently deceased mother's things. She discovered a big purple storage tub filled with her mother's journal writings and correspondence.

One box was filled with unsent letters and cards to Chad.

Over and over again Darla's mom had written prayerful notes to her unmet grandson, telling him how loved he was, and how she and Darla were praying for him every day . . . just as they'd promised.

Reflections

For two decades Darla was unable to physically embrace her son Chad . . . but through the prayers that she, and her mom, were saying for him every day . . . she could imagine herself hugging him.

From that secret place where petitions for her son were lifted up to the Lord — in her heart — she prayed for Chad to have a happy and fruitful life and for God to lead her firstborn son back to her.

Hindsight shows us that Chad's burning question — *Was I loved?* — became his motivation to seek her. That, plus the prayers of Darla and Dolores, was what God needed to divinely align Chad's path back to his mother's arms.

Every child is a blessing and a gift from God.

Darla honored God by choosing to give birth to Chad, and allowing him to be adopted by a good family. In return, God honored Darla by reuniting her with the baby she once smothered in kisses and kept in loving prayer for twenty-one years.

> Children are a heritage from the Lord,
> The fruit of the womb is a reward.
> — Psalm 127:3 (NKJV)

1D
Tina — Moms Pray, God Listens

Tina Culleton, a devoted mother of faith, was inspired by a Christian Women's Conference to pray for her children — not just in the present but for the future marriages of each child, and that they would be rooted in God's love and grace.

So, when Tina's three sons and her daughter, Katelynn, were still in diapers, she began praying for their future spouses.

Tina met her own husband, Marty, while both were in the military stationed in Italy. She retired when they started having children.

Military families are always on the move. Tina embraced the adventure from Italy to Kansas, Maine to Florida, and Germany to Texas. But it was always a challenge for her to find the right school situation for her kids.

One day, while newly stationed in Frankfurt, Germany, Tina and the family ventured off to a smaller nearby US military base thirty minutes away at Wiesbaden to check out their PX (post exchange).

While standing in line to pay for lunch, Tina struck up a conversation with another American military mother. In the space of moments they discovered they both had much in common. The woman had three boys of roughly the same ages as Tina's children and was also homeschooling them. Also, Tina discovered that the other mother was a believer who, like her, prayed regularly for her children's future spouses.

The two of them talked about getting their kids together for a homeschooling date, causing Tina to enthusiastically dig for her address book for the lady to write down her name and number. Tina kept a different address book for each place they lived.

On her way home she made a mental note to call the other mother, but life got busy and Marty received new orders to return stateside. Soon the Culletons were settled in San Antonio, Texas, where Tina was finally able to pursue a lifelong dream — studying and launching a career in nursing.

She loved every minute of it. However, her demanding schedule made it impossible to continue homeschooling the kids. So she transitioned her children to public school.

When it came time for her daughter, Katelynn, to attend high school, the boys urged their parents to find her a different school than the one they attended. It was *way* too rough, they thought, for their baby sister.

So Katelynn was enrolled in a nearby Christian high school, where she thrived, joining the basketball and volleyball teams as well as singing competitively. She also began singing worship music at the church next to her school.

One day, while Tina sat in her car, waiting to pick up Katelynn from volleyball practice, she noticed a handsome boy in khakis and a green polo shirt walking to his car.

"Do you see that boy?" Tina asked Katelynn excitedly as she entered the car. "That's exactly who I see in my mind when I pray for your husband!"

Katelynn rolled her eyes at her mother's comment, knowing full well that Tina had been praying for her perfect husband since she was in onesies.

"Mom . . . you know I have a boyfriend."

Yes, Tina did know. But she wasn't convinced that "the one" had come along yet for her daughter. So, she just kept on praying.

One summer day after Katelynn graduated, Tina was finishing up laundry when the doorbell rang.

She was shocked as she opened the door to see that she was face-to-face with the "khakis and green shirt" guy! She recognized him instantly.

What on earth can he be here for? she wondered.

"Hello, ma'am," he said politely. "I'm Oliver Schlotfeldt. I'm here to tell Katelynn goodbye before I leave for the Marines."

Though Tina was astounded, she didn't want to interrogate the poor kid. But she did offer him a seat while she went to get Katelynn.

"Thank you but no, ma'am. The man of the house isn't here, so I better not take a seat."

His manners blew her away.

What Tina came to learn later was this . . .

A few years earlier, after Hurricane Katrina wreaked havoc on the Gulf Coast, Katelynn went on a mission trip with her youth group to help with cleanup and reconstruction.

Initially, it was mostly girls who signed up

for the trip from her school, none of whom had experience working with a hammer or construction tools. So to help, Katelynn's principal volunteered two strapping teenage boys from the church associated with the school — which he also pastored — one of whom was Oliver.

Though shy at first, he and Katelynn became close.

Katelynn was impressed that Oliver already had a sense of who he was and what he wanted. When he turned eighteen, he planned to enroll in the Marines and attend language school as a linguist like his father.

Besides Katelynn's beauty — which was obvious — Oliver appreciated the ease with which she expressed her faith during the youth group's nightly debriefings.

In fact, they were the two who spoke up the most during those sessions . . . an obvious connection each of them tucked away.

However, once back home from Katrina cleanup, their schooling and activities provided little opportunity for contact. Oliver, who attended public high school, was very active as a commandant in the school's JROTC program and commander of the Varsity Armed Drill Team. And he only visited Katelynn's Christian high school when it had something to do with his church next door.

Also, both were dating other people.

A while later, Oliver's church and Katelynn's school had an annual function in which both organizations participated.

They needed volunteers to dress up as those in the era of Jesus for an event called "Christmas City," well-known around San Antonio.

That's how Katelynn and Oliver began socializing as friends prior to graduation . . . and how . . . a week before Oliver left for basic training . . . he showed up on Tina's doorstep to tell Katelynn goodbye.

Over the next six months, Katelynn and Oliver ended their other relationships and — to Tina's delight — finally started dating over the phone while Oliver was by then stationed in California, attending the prestigious Department of Defense Language Institute to learn Arabic.

That was December.

By June they were engaged . . . and were to be married the following December . . . as they no longer could stand being apart!

Tina was overwhelmed with joy. Oliver was faithful, well-mannered, and respectful. A man of deliberate and intentional faith. He was everything Tina prayed for her daughter right from the time she was a toddler.

When the couple's parents met, they all got along famously. In fact, Tina and Laura Schlotfeldt, Oliver's mom, looked at each other, unable to shake the feeling that they'd previously met.

But try as they might — Tina asking "Were you ever a patient at my medical center?" or Laura asking "Did you ever go to such and such women's conference?" — they couldn't recall when or where that might have been. So they chalked it up to déjà vu.

Within days of Katelynn and Oliver's wedding, there was a bit of a hiccup with Oliver's approved military leave — only twenty-four hours before the wedding everyone was still left hanging. Would Oliver be there?

In the end, it was granted, with Oliver arriving back home just in time for the festivities.

It was a wonderful ceremony! Katelynn, the only girl in a family with three brothers, had a beautiful, Texas-size wedding against a backdrop of real Texas Longhorn cattle, a running brook, and her favorite colors — turquoise and chocolate brown — creating a beautiful décor with draping pearls and stunning flowers everywhere.

"Thank you, Lord," prayed Tina gratefully. "Oliver is *the* exact man I prayed for my daughter!"

But . . . it wasn't until sometime later . . . that God revealed His entire game plan.

As Tina was sorting through some old moving boxes one day, she came across all the old address books from early in her marriage, from base to base and city to city.

Flipping through one of them nostalgically, she perused the names of old friends and acquaintances. When she opened it to the S section Tina stopped cold.

There plain as day was the name and number for . . . Laura Schlotfeldt!

Oliver's mom!

A memory finally flashed into view . . . from two decades before . . . Tina handing the address book to a lady in line at the food court near the PX, asking her to write down her name . . . so their kids might have a homeschool get-together.

Tina was shocked! That action was initiated as a result of both mothers sharing that they had prayed for the future marriages of their little kids!

If confirmed . . . this would be an astounding Godwink! she thought.

Tina quickly called Oliver's mother, Laura.

It *was* confirmed!

Tina Culleton and Laura Schlotfeldt — their families stationed in Germany at the same time, on different bases — realized that their prayers for their children's future spouses . . . were never forgotten by God!

Not only that, but He played matchmaker, bringing Katelynn and Oliver together in what can only be called one hugely romantic, divinely aligned Godwink!

REFLECTIONS

The most important decision our children will make, apart from their decision to follow Christ, is whom they choose to marry.

Yet in all matters, and especially this one, a mother's prayer is a secret weapon the Lord will use!

When moms pray, God goes to work.

It was a double dose of prayer when Tina and Laura both petitioned the Lord to guide their children to a Godly partner who would love and honor Him and each other.

Some might say it was a random encounter whereby both Tina and Laura happened to be in the same line, at the same time, striking up a conversation about praying for their young children's future mates. But with God there are no random encounters, nor happenstances, nor coincidences.

Those mothers' prayers were lined up perfectly for Katelynn and Oliver to intersect — or as we say, to be divinely aligned — at God's appointed time. He prepared the hearts of those future spouses before they were even born.

> Before I formed you in the womb
> I knew you,
> And before you were born
> I consecrated you. . . .
>
> JEREMIAH 1:5 (NASB)

2
Moving On After Losing My Mom

2A
Jonna — Mom's Red Roses

Her kitchen was filled with the sweet smell of roses.

Eddie Ruth Fitzgerald filled a mason jar with the beautiful red blooms she had just cut from one of the many rosebushes in her yard in Flint, Texas — not far from Tyler, the "Rose Capital of the World." She preferred to admire them outside where they belonged, so this was a rare treat.

She was placing the jar on the counter when the phone rang. It was her daughter, Jonna Fitzgerald, a former Miss Texas and Miss America runner-up. The two were best friends and shared a special relationship. It was not unusual for them to talk three or four times a day, discussing anything from her roses and favorite recipes to Jonna's beau, Garrett.

Eddie Ruth liked Garrett. He was quick to lend her a helping hand and they would kid with each other. She spoke openly and fondly about his "mischievous little boy" characteristics.

Whenever he paid her a visit he'd playfully ask, "Do you have any candy?" knowing full well she kept a candy dish always at the ready.

She'd reward his silliness with candy and a laugh.

Eddie Ruth signed off on her call to Jonna with "I'm going to putter around in the garden."

The garden was her happy place, where she tended her roses and the dogs she adored. She was always trying different techniques to help her flowers grow, like adding food scraps or coffee grounds to the soil. But the real secret to her success in growing beautiful blossoms — those in her yard and those for her very own Miss Texas — was her loving and caring spirit.

Another of her secrets was that, in later years, she sometimes "enhanced" her and Jonna's rose gardens with silk flowers from the Dollar Store. She explained with a laugh, "They blend right in . . . and they sure last longer!"

When Eddie Ruth's health began to fail, Jonna was distraught over the thought of losing her precious mother.

A week before she died, Jonna wished for a way to keep her mother's voice and family stories close to her after she passed.

She bought an inexpensive micro recorder at the local drugstore. At the hospice, surrounded by her loving family, Jonna asked her mom questions about her life and recorded her answers.

Jonna was a little frustrated with the digital recorder. To turn it on, she had to hold down the power button for a few seconds and then push a recessed play button with her fingernail. It was designed this way so it wouldn't accidentally turn itself on.

She stuffed it in the side pocket of her briefcase, stored it in the hatchback of her car, and put it out of mind.

Eddie Ruth died in hospice a week later.

At her mother's memorial service, Jonna displayed beautiful spring roses from her mom's garden. It was a lovely remembrance of her mother, and, as one might imagine, her roses moved family and friends to tears.

On Easter Sunday a week later, Jonna and Garrett were on their way to church. Because they had stopped for coffee with Garrett's parents in a nearby town, Garrett was driving when something caught his eye on a small side street. He was moved to slow the car to a stop to take another look.

"Did you see those roses?!"

Jonna had not. There was no traffic, so Garrett put the car in reverse.

Seconds later Jonna was gazing at the magnificent red rosebushes lining the short lane. They were beautiful . . . just like her mom's.

At that moment they heard a voice . . . speaking from the back seat! A woman's voice, filling the car with soft-spoken and loving words!

Jonna was speechless.

"That sounds like your mother!" said Garrett.

"It *is* my mother!"

"How can that be?" they shouted in unison.

Garrett threw the car in park as they both jumped out and looked curiously into the back seat.

The voice was still speaking.

"Garrett, we are both hearing my mother speaking in our car . . . or we're both crazy!" she said.

■ ■ ■ ■

Garrett quickly moved to the rear of the car and opened the hatchback. But . . . there was no evidence of a source.

Then . . . Jonna figured it out. The voice must be Eddie Ruth's . . . recorded a week or two ago.

"Check the recorder . . . I think I put it in my briefcase."

There it was . . . playing for them. Jonna grabbed it. Deftly using her fingernail, she turned it off

With puzzled looks they concluded that the recorder — purposely made difficult to use, so it wouldn't turn itself on — somehow had.

"It's a confirmation . . ." she whispered, with a slight smile at Garrett. "I was feeling a little lack of closure today . . . but now I know. She's in heaven. I'm okay. Everything is okay."

Her soul was flooded with peace and comfort.

The couple looked at each other — teary-eyed and laughing at the same time — joyfully collapsing into each other's arms.

POSTSCRIPT

Time passed . . . Jonna and Garrett were married in a beautiful ceremony.

They were blessed to have Garrett's parents in attendance, while Jonna's parents were there in spirit with a loving tribute.

The ceremony hall was covered in roses — red for Eddie Ruth and yellow for Miss Texas. The bluebonnet look-alikes were for her father, Truman "Blue" Fitzgerald, nicknamed for his striking blue eyes.

Jonna also carried a locket in her bridal bouquet. On one side was a photo of her parents on their wedding day. On the other, a photo of them on their fiftieth anniversary. Theirs was a love to last.

Not long ago, Jonna and Garrett sold Eddie Ruth's home — the ranch where Jonna grew up. But just before they did, Garrett, the kind and thoughtful son-in-law, moved some of the rosebushes to their own yard for Jonna to enjoy.

Now their kitchen is filled with a real treat — the delightful and comforting scent of her sweet mother's roses, a reminder of her forever love.

Reflections

The flowers appear on the earth,
the time of singing has come. . . .
— Song of Solomon 2:12 (NKJV)

Eddie Ruth found joy in her garden and the glory of God's creation. She shared that joy with Jonna, Garrett, and those she loved . . . even after her death.

If you're grieving the loss of a mother, sister, daughter, or a friend, let Eddie Ruth's spirit speak to you as well.

While we miss them terribly, the love we shared never dies.

Each spring the season of Resurrection is yours to celebrate. It's time to revel in the rebirth of nature. It blooms again. Gloriously. Beautifully.

It is annual evidence of God's presence in your life, all around you, every day.

2B
Katherine and Diana — Is Hope Lost?

The Hope Diamond is perhaps the most famous diamond in the world. It's exquisite, priceless, and shines with a brightness unmatched by any other.

That's exactly how Diana Himmelstein would have described her late mother, whose name was Hope.

Now, standing in her bedroom in the clear morning sunlight, Diana was admiring her dear mother's diamond ring that had been bequeathed to her.

No, it wasn't 44 carats like the historic gem on display at the Smithsonian Institution, but her mother's engagement ring meant the world to Diana.

It's incredibly beautiful, she thought, *but, even more important, it keeps Mother close to me.*

Diana was about to slip the ring on her finger when she stopped to rub on some hand cream.

One of the many things she and her mother shared was the shape of their hands — skinny fingers with bigger knuckles. So the springed metal ring-size adjuster inside the band that fit her mother also fit her perfectly.

Giving the lotion a moment to dry, Diana enjoyed the soothing scent and then set the ring down near her purse before zipping off in mom mode to get her two sons ready for the day.

She glanced at her watch. They were running late.

She took a few steps downstairs and called out, "Hurry up, boys! It's time to go."

Even though it was a school vacation day, they had plans that morning to go to a trampoline center in a little plaza on Armour Street in West Town, on the north side of Chicago.

The boys ran out the door to get in the car and she quickly grabbed her purse and headed out behind them.

If only it was this easy to get them out the door for school!

Several blocks away, Katherine Gloede was still in deep mourning over the loss of her father, Ben Plominski. He had died from glioblastoma, a rare brain cancer.

Her dad was her hero — a brilliant electrical engineer who emigrated from communist Poland in the seventies. He met and married her mother, Barbara, a Polish table tennis champion, and started a business working as an electrician to provide for his family. He was a proud American with a zest for life.

Just by observing the way he lived, Katherine learned the value of working hard for what she wanted and the importance of always doing the right thing.

Some of Katherine's grief found expression in anxiety about her husband Dan's health. She loved him so much, and she couldn't bear the idea of anything happening to him too.

Dan was under extraordinary stress at work. There were some significant, unexpected challenges at his new job. She pleaded with him to see a doctor for a checkup.

The doctor advised Dan to start working out with a personal trainer whom he highly recommended, located in a little plaza on Armour Street in West Town.

As the boys tried to see who could jump the highest on the trampoline, Diana spotted Danielle and Becky, mothers of children her boys knew. She hadn't seen them in months.

As they chatted about the latest things going on with the kids, Diana glanced down at her hand and realized that in the rush of getting out of the house she had forgotten to put on her ring. No problem. She would put it on when she got home.

The rising sun colored the edges of the sky with the most majestic hues as Dan arrived for his first session with the personal trainer. He pulled into the lot behind a small L-shaped plaza of old brick buildings that housed several businesses, including a trampoline center.

He kept going to the end of the plaza and parked in front of the gym.

As he got out of the car, his phone rang. It was work. Ugh. So much for this gym time being a stress reliever.

Dan took the call in the parking lot and paced. Back and forth. Back and forth. Right alongside a large and smelly trash dumpster. Ugh, again.

Then he stopped, put a hand to his head in complete and utter frustration, ended the call, and looked down.

Something sparkled against the pavement.

He looked more closely, bending down to

pick it up. It was a ring.

He couldn't tell if it was a toy, a fake, or the real deal. But it was damaged. It looked like it had been run over by a car.

Why would this beautiful ring be near a dumpster? he wondered.

He didn't have time to worry about one more thing, so he entered the gym and gave the ring to the receptionist to put in their lost and found.

Diana was in tears.

She couldn't find her mother's ring! She knew it had to be in the house somewhere. And she looked everywhere.

She moved furniture. She went through trash cans. Opened closets, cabinets, and drawers. She turned the house upside down. Nothing. She looked in the same places, over and over. Then even looked in odd places — like the refrigerator.

She retraced her morning steps, in her mind, recalling she was rushed, and distracted by her boys' excitement to get to the trampoline place.

Panic crept over her. The feelings of devastation. Her mother's diamond ring was priceless!

Ending his workout, and on his way to

work, Dan called Katherine and mentioned the ring he'd found.

The lawyer in her came out, and she told him he needed to go back and get the ring.

"I have too much on my plate right now to deal with this, Katherine. If you want to look for the owner, I'll go back and get it. But I'm one hundred percent not getting involved!"

"We're already involved. Go back and get the ring. Don't worry. I'll take care of it."

"How are you going to do that?"

"I don't know. But I know I will."

He knew better than to doubt her. He turned the car around and headed back to the gym.

For weeks, Diana searched for her ring. She grew more and more desperate as days and weeks passed.

Though it had been several years since her mother died, she missed her every day. Now it felt like she was losing her all over again.

She believed the ring was in her house, but she had to consider the possibility she had somehow lost it at the trampoline center. That was the only place she had gone that day.

The woman who answered the phone at

the trampoline center checked their lost and found. Nothing. She took down Diana's information and promised to share it with the rest of the staff. But nobody called.

When Katherine held the ring her husband had found, she knew in her heart it meant a great deal to someone. The broken metal size adjuster in the damaged band suggested to her it was passed down, perhaps from mother to daughter.

And she felt that somehow she was getting heavenly assistance in this endeavor to do the right thing and to find the ring's rightful owner.

She FaceTimed her godfather, a retired jeweler in Florida, who told her how to clean the ring. But, just by viewing it, via the internet, he doubted it was real.

Real or fake didn't matter to Katherine — she suspected it might be special to someone — and doing the right thing, that's what mattered.

But . . . she took it to a jeweler to find out, anyway.

The answer made Katherine's jaw drop.

It *was* real. And worth thirty thousand dollars!

■ ■ ■ ■

Optimism was fading for Diana.

Her mother's ring might be lost forever.

Looking through Hope's papers, she discovered that her mother had the engagement ring reset twice since Gary, her beloved husband of forty-two years, had given it to her in the early seventies.

Diana would need the most recent appraisal to provide the most exact description, in order to file an insurance claim and to make a replica.

She called several jewelers in the Philadelphia area to try to locate where her mother had her ring reset, but with no success.

On the morning of her fortieth birthday, Diana woke up thinking *that* was the day she was going to have heavenly help with the ring. She just knew it.

That afternoon, a thought popped into her mind: there was one more jewelry store located close to her parents' home.

She called them — and they had her mother's records! A full appraisal and description of the ring. Every detail!

With this information, she knew she could get the funds from the insurance company and have her mother's lost ring re-created.

What a birthday gift, she thought. Though her precious ring was gone, creating an exact likeness would be the next-best thing.

Katherine dug in. Many people knew her reputation for being determined. So it was time to double down on trying to find the ring's owner.

She filed a police report. She appraised and even insured the ring, just in case she needed additional information, or something happened to it before the owner was found.

She posted on every social media group she thought could be relevant. Several people responded, claiming the ring might be theirs.

It wasn't.

And even though he "wasn't going to get involved," Dan admired Katherine's quest and wanted to be supportive.

Every week he asked at the gym if anyone had reported losing a ring. No one had.

He made the rounds, several times, of each business in the shared lot — not only the gym, but the brewery and the trampoline place. No luck. No one he talked with knew anything about a lost ring being reported.

Friends and coworkers told Katherine to

give it up.

You did the best you could. It's impossible. A needle in a haystack. Finders keepers.

But Katherine persisted. The search gave her real purpose and refocused her attention away from the grief for her dad that was lurking just beneath the surface.

She believed with her whole heart that the spirit of her father was on this mission with her, and together they would succeed. His voice spoke to her heart the loudest.

Don't give up.

At 9:44 on a morning in June, the replacement ring arrived at Diana's front door.

She opened the package and held the replica of her mother's ring.

It was beautiful, yes. But . . . it made her cry.

It looked like her mother's ring, but . . . it wasn't *really* her mother's ring.

Minutes later, eighteen to be exact, Diana missed a call on her cell phone.

At Katherine's request, Dan made the rounds a third time at the businesses in the lot where he found the ring.

When he went into the trampoline place,

there was a different person working at the entrance. He asked her — now by rote — if anyone had reported a lost ring.

"Let me check our lost-and-found log."

A "lost-and-found log"? Interesting, no one mentioned that, during the various times I was here.

"Yes, it looks like a Diana Himmelstein lost a ring in April."

"Can I get her contact information?"

"Sure."

She read it aloud as he entered it into his phone.

Inside he was excited. *Katherine will be thrilled to have a new lead!*

Later in the day, he would share the contact information with his wife so she could follow up with the woman — Diana Himmelstein — after work. For now he used his foolproof method for saving a number to his phone — he dialed it and then immediately hung up.

Eighteen is an important number in the Jewish faith. It means "chai" or "life." And it is considered to be very good luck.

Exactly eighteen minutes elapsed between the delivery of Diana's new ring and the missed call on her phone!

She never returned missed calls. She presumed they were all spam.

But suddenly she found herself calling back a number she didn't recognize.

A man's surprised voice answered. He wasn't expecting her to call back and mentioned something about a lost ring.

Stunned, Diana cried out to this unknown caller, "DID YOU FIND MY RING?!"

The man told her he found a ring in the parking lot near the trampoline center in April.

She was breathless. It had to be supernatural! It *must* be her ring!

He explained that he and his wife would need proof, of course.

He provided his email, and she recognized his name — Dan Gloede! (*Really?*) Diana had actually met him through a business acquaintance years before!

Katherine was now the guardian of a thirty-thousand-dollar ring. She could not give it to the wrong person. She had to be 100 percent certain that this person, named Diana, was indeed the ring's owner.

The appraisal Diana emailed to them appeared to match, but she still had questions.

Katherine and Dan scheduled a time to speak with Diana in person.

■ ■ ■ ■

"What's an identifying feature about this ring?" Katherine asked.

Diana rattled off clarity, cut, and size. All very specific and technical details from the appraisal. She wanted to be precise but also wanted them to believe her.

"Yes, but what about it . . . could *only* be yours?"

Diana couldn't think of what she meant. There was nothing engraved in the band or anything like that. How could she prove that it was hers? Under pressure, it was hard for her to think straight.

Then it came to Diana in a flash. The fit. Like Cinderella and the slipper. The metal ring adjuster inside the band. The thing she and her mother shared — knuckles bigger than their skinny fingers! Her eyes widened. She blurted what came to mind.

"There's a little device inside the ring . . . to adjust the fit around the knuckles!"

"That's it!"

Like a lost treasure, Katherine gently placed Hope's ring into Diana's hand.

Diana held it gingerly. It was damaged — bent from being run over by a car — but it was her mother's ring, and Diana was overjoyed to hold it again.

Diana and Katherine looked at each other and both cried happy tears of relief.

Once the tension was over, Diana and Katherine allowed themselves to be instant friends.

Katherine felt a compulsion to speak about some of the things she'd discovered during her detective work, including from friends and family who helped her along the way.

"Himmelstein means 'stone from heaven,' " she shared with a laugh.

"It is indeed!" replied Diana.

"Something else is amazing," said Katherine, pausing to reveal another Godwink with the utmost of respect. "While reading your mother's obituary in the *Philadelphia Inquirer,* I began to wonder, *What was your mother's cause of death?* And then the answer was right there in black and white. Glioblastoma."

Diana was nodding in agreement as Katherine was readying the incredible clincher.

"*That* is same rare cancer *my father* died from! There are only thirteen thousand cases diagnosed in the United States every year!"

"Wow," they said in unison, under their breaths.

They marveled that perhaps someday they would understand that the journey they had both been divinely led to pursue may have been for a greater purpose than a lost ring!

"We'll just have to see," mused Katherine.

Diana was still trying to process the earlier revelation: "Both of us have been grieving the loss of a beloved parent . . . who died from the same rare disease," said Diana with wonder. "What are the odds?"

POSTSCRIPT

The ring setting was beyond repair, but Diana was told it was "a miracle" that her "Hope's Diamond" was neither chipped nor damaged in any way.

While sending a reimbursement check to the insurance company, Diana had her jeweler return the diamond from the replacement ring but kept the new setting.

He then put Hope's diamond in the new setting — just like the original, with a metal ring-size adjuster inside the band!

In the following years, blessings abounded for both Katherine and Dan, including new career opportunities and unexpected bonuses. Were they connected to the ring? Only heaven knows.

But finding and returning Hope's ring gave Katherine the best gift ever — a feeling of closeness with the memory of her father and tremendous peace and comfort during her time of grief.

It's like he sent a postcard from heaven to say he arrived safely, and everything is okay.

Reflections

But this I call to mind, and therefore I have hope:
The steadfast love of the Lord never ceases;
his mercies never come to an end;
they are new every morning. . . .
— Lamentations 3:21–32 (ESV)

When Diana's mother was diagnosed with glioblastoma, she was given fifteen months, but with incredible strength and positivity, her family was blessed to have Hope for over five more years.

Diana said, "Even after she passed, I felt a sense of Hope for Life. Even when the worst possible things happen, it's still going to be okay."

And isn't that exactly what a Godwink is?

Feelings of love from above? And hugs?

We're wishing hugs and Godwinks for each of you reading this!

2C
Virginia — New Mom's Surprise

Virginia Haworth Berg fondly remembers her mom, Kathy, as a faithful and spiritual woman, always looking for signs . . . God-winks . . . in random objects, license plates, or two-dollar bills.

For her, these "signs of hope" always confirmed that she was on the right path.

There was that Mother's Day brunch, for instance, with Mom and Virginia's sister Savannah. While paying the tab Mom was handed her change. She looked down and saw two — not one, but two — two-dollar bills.

She got all excited, shouting, "This has to be a sign!"

As confirmation, she pulled a pencil from her purse and scrawled the date — May 9, 2010 — on each bill and told her daughters to keep them as a memory of that special Mother's Day together.

■ ■ ■ ■

A few years later when her mother was in failing health, from debilitating cancer, Virginia tried to come to terms with the prospect of not having her mom in her daily life. She was saddened that Mom would never meet her future husband nor any of their children.

Virginia expressed those regrets in their final conversation. She recalls her mom smiling slightly just before closing her eyes for the last time, saying weakly, "If only I could have one more sunset with you."

In that moment of grief and loss, Virginia witnessed the terrible unfairness in the passages in life.

Yet she was grateful to have witnessed her mother's optimism and unwavering faith. She sensed she would somehow remain connected to her . . . perhaps through those "signs" Mom always saw everywhere . . . Godwinks.

After the funeral, Virginia downloaded a copy of the book *When God Winks,* hoping it would help her process her grief. It did. "It brought me so much peace and comfort," she told her sister.

■ ■ ■ ■

A few years later, Virginia was happily married to Charlie Berg and feeling the joy of expecting her second baby. A weekend getaway with the love of her life seemed perfectly timed just before the new baby's arrival.

At dinner, listening to romantic music and watching the sunset sparkle on the water, Charlie opened his wallet to tip the band.

"Oh, by the way, I found this in that pile of papers you asked me to shred," said Charlie, handing her a two-dollar bill.

Virginia stared at it, then burst into tears.

"What's the matter? It's just a two-dollar bill!"

"It's not just any two-dollar bill!" said Virginia. "Mom gave me this on Mother's Day. See?"

She showed him the date, May 9, 2010, written in her mom's handwriting!

"Oh my gosh." . . . It dawned on her . . . "Maybe my prayer to have Mom's knack for seeing Godwink signs is being answered!"

Then she cried out, "Charlie, look! Over the water . . . it's a spectacular sunset just like Mom requested. Those were her last words!"

She looked down, first at her swollen midsection . . . due any day . . . then at the two-dollar bill in her hand . . . in her mother's writing . . . and connected the dots. This wasn't just any weekend . . . it was Mother's Day weekend! And it was only days before their first daughter would be born.

She jumped up, threw her arms around Charlie, and hugged him tightly, whispering, "I think God just fulfilled Mom's dying wish . . . to have one last sunset together. And *my* wish, to have her meet you and our babies."

They held on to that hug for what seemed like minutes.

Mom's philosophy made sense . . . Godwinks happen to everyone. We just need to develop the eyes to see them.

Reflections

Virginia wanted to see God's signs but perhaps felt her faith was not strong enough to identify the Godwinks in the way her mother had.

Yet, recognizing the nonverbal voice of

God improves with practice. The more we seek Him, the more we'll find Him, the Bible tells us. And the more we see Godwinks, the more we see them.

Make it a daily habit to look for the divine dots in your life and you'll soon realize that God's handiwork is aligning you to be at the right place at the right time for the outcome He wants you to have.

Every Godwink is a person-to-person communication, especially for you, out of eight billion people on the planet.

Doesn't it make your heart leap to know how special you are in God's eyes? He desires to give you signs of hope to lift your spirits just when you need it most.

That's what He did for Virginia and that is what He will do for you!

> Aren't two sparrows sold for a penny?
> Yet not one of them falls to the ground
> without your Father's consent.
> — MATTHEW 10:29 (CSB)

2D
Ginger — Missing My Mom

The soft blue glow of the computer screen illuminated Ginger's face as she stared intently at the endless list of Amazon products. It was like looking for a needle in a haystack.

Darn. If I could only remember the name of the book.

She smiled at the thought of her mother's delight the day Ginger gave her that book.

She had compulsively bought it online because it contained the kind of home remedies Mom grew up with in East Texas and loved to spout with a twinkle in her eye, such as "The best cure for a bee sting is a wad of tobacco!"

"Of course, you might want ta chew it a little . . . first," she would add with a wry smile.

"Heck! Who could remember the title of a book from fifteen years ago! And Mom — the only person who could tell me — has now gone to live with you, God!"

Each book title Ginger scrolled through might as well have been written in Greek, because she had no idea what the title even started with.

She didn't even understand why the book had come to mind, out of thin air. Maybe it was as simple as her missing her mom.

Yes! That was for sure.

It is never easy to lose a loved one, but nothing could prepare Ginger for the anguish of losing her mother. The memories came flooding back. The heartache that never seemed to stop.

"She was a good mom."

That's how Ginger put it when anyone asked about her mother at the service.

She loved and admired her mom. They had a great relationship — for the most part. Even though the last few years were more difficult than she cared to admit.

Almost as hard as losing a parent was watching the person you love wilt under the debilitating weight of dementia.

To see the strong woman she'd known all her life suffer with confusion and failing health was all the more straining to their relationship when her mother's mental deterioration caused a contentiousness toward her.

Ginger didn't blame her mother . . . it was the dementia. But she hated the illness that stole the wonderful woman her mother once was.

If only I could have that *woman back.*

Then out loud, to no one but herself and God, Ginger resolutely announced, "If I could only have you back for one minute, Mom, I'd let you know how much I still love you and miss you."

She quickly assessed that she was sitting there staring at a computer screen, trying to grasp the name of a book that once gave them lots of laughs together.

Was she seeking a bridge back to that witty woman whom Ginger missed so much . . . who lived there till just a couple of weeks ago?

Mom had gone on to heaven two Thursdays before. The funeral was last week. A beautiful send-off — a testament to her mother's devotion to God and a lifetime of pouring herself out for the sake of her children.

Back to the book. Whatever happened to it anyway?

A string of thoughts passed through Ginger's mind, ending with *Mom probably gave it to someone at church. That was like her.*

After scrolling through a few more pages on Amazon, Ginger decided to bite the bullet and just place an order.

She found a book that, to the best of her knowledge, fit the topic of home remedies — now ashamed she'd wasted this much time looking through, what, a hundred books? She quickly punched the "add to cart" button.

She did notice it had said "good" when describing the condition of the book. Maybe that was why it was cheaper . . . it wasn't brand-new.

Who cares. Done.

A week later, a package arrived wrapped in typical Amazon fashion. Picking it up from the doorstep, Ginger took it inside and tossed it on the couch until she had more time to focus.

As the evening sky began to dim and night pulled its blanket up across her neighborhood, Ginger sat down to inspect the package.

What was she hoping for?

Well, best-case scenario was that she had picked out a book that came close in content to the one that had provided Ginger and her mom so many laughs. And just maybe, those laughs would make her feel better.

Pulling open the package, she held the book in her hands. It was a little worn, but pretty well cared for. She was grateful for that.

Opening it up, she thumbed through the pages. She could almost smell the concoction of remedies and their unique fragrances.

As she flipped through the pages, something dropped out and fluttered to the floor. Bending down, she scooped it up and turned it over in her palm.

What's this?

She could hardly believe what she was seeing — a note! In a handwriting that was unmistakably familiar.

It was her mom's writing! It said:

My Granny made lye soap from butter . . .
It smelled to high heavens!

A bolt of excitement and disbelief shot through her as she flipped through more pages. Another note fell out. And then another!

Her heart raced. It was like a treasure trove of secrets directly from Mom.

It was a genuine Godwink. Despite all the

heartbreak that her mother's dementia had left her with, these were notes written by Mom when she was full of vim and vigor!

With the help of God, and just after she'd wished her healthy mom was back for just one minute, she was sitting there reading notes written in her mother's own hand.

It was the healing moment Ginger needed, and it was done in a way that could only have been designed by God.

He moved a forgotten book from a lonely bookshelf in a store somewhere across the World Wide Web and back into the hands of a daughter who very much needed to know that her mom still loved her.

Reflections

Those handwritten notes had a whole new meaning after Ginger's mom graduated to heaven.

So often after losing a loved one, we find it's the little things we savor most. God wants to remind us of the mystery in the mundane.

It was a blessed assurance that their hearts will always be connected and one day they will be reunited again.

So you have sorrow now,
but I will see you again; then you will

rejoice,
and no one can rob you of that joy.
— JOHN 16:22 (NLT)

3
Like a Second Mom to Me

3A
Kathy Bee — Footprints in the Sand

God graced young Kathy Bee with a beautiful voice.

At twenty, she was about to embark on an exciting cross-country tour to share her gift of song with others. Her only problem? Leaving the mother she adored and the family she loved in the village of Bloomingburg, Ohio.

Her small bag was packed and sitting by the door.

She and her mom sat nervously on the couch in the front room, both doing their best not to break out in tears, to trigger the other.

Kathy's mother took her hand.

"I'm so proud of you . . . so happy for you. Now . . . God is going to have you dazzle everybody . . . not just us!"

Kathy tried to say thanks. But for once, her voice failed her. She moved her lower lip above her top lip and just nodded.

Beep-beep.

A van filled with musicians, playing a loud radio, swerved into the family's driveway.

Kathy stood up. Her mother crushed her in a warm embrace, not wanting to let go. When she did, she slipped something the size of a small calling card into her daughter's hand.

Kathy found her voice. "What's this?"

"A poem. 'Footprints in the Sand.' Whenever you feel alone . . . just read it. It'll remind you that you're *never* alone."

"Thank you, Mom. I love you!"

She gave her mother a kiss on the cheek and was out the door . . . on her way.

As the van headed south over the county line, Kathy watched the familiar landscape passing away and then looked down at the little card . . . as three lines popped out at her.

. . . I noticed footprints in the sand . . .
Sometimes there were two sets of
  footprints.
Other times there was one set of
  footprints.

And farther down . . .

Why, when I needed you most,

Have you not been there for me?

Kathy knew this was a poem that she'd be reading over and over.

In fact, it felt as though it was written especially for her!

That's why Mom gave it to me, she thought, smiling slightly, realizing that the landscape was now totally unfamiliar. And she was already missing Mom.

Then two tiny words at the bottom of the poem on the card caught Kathy's eye:

Author Unknown

Who writes something so beautiful and never claims it? She tucked the card into her wallet, where it would never leave.

Two years later.

Mary Stevenson, a somewhat eccentric blond-haired woman in her fifties, made her way into the Palomino Club in North Hollywood, California, where she was a regular.

A former dancer herself, she always felt inspired by the variety of talent that graced the Palomino Club stage, week in and week out. She was eager to see the newcomers to the business . . . and she loved to shower them with support.

Nodding to familiar waitstaff with a bright smile, she made her way through the crowd, took a seat at her usual table in the back, and waited for the show to begin.

Offstage, Kathy Bee could hardly contain her excitement. Since she'd left Ohio, she had made her way in Los Angeles and recorded with a popular band.

Now she really felt good about herself because she'd been invited to perform live at the legendary Palomino Club on Lankershim Boulevard, where so many other country artists had gotten their break!

Checking herself in the mirror, she was pleased with her outfit, a beautiful flowing yellow-and-black chiffon gown.

She said a little prayer: "God, please let me knock it out of the park with this song."

When it was time, she walked confidently to the stage, turned to the band, and said matter-of-factly, " 'Blue Bayou' in the key of B-flat."

Within moments her moving rendition of the Roy Orbison song, made famous by Linda Ronstadt, had the audience eating out of her hand. Most were moving in sync with the music or singing along.

Here and there she could see a few tears welling up. That was good . . . she was touching hearts.

When her song was finished, it took her a little time to make her way offstage and through the sea of appreciative new fans stopping her, getting her autograph, en route to the table that had been reserved for talent.

When she finally took her seat and relaxed, she felt a tap on her shoulder. She turned to see her biggest new fan of all: a woman in her fifties with a beaming smile.

"You're beautiful! You have a fantastic voice . . . and 'Blue Bayou' is one of my all-time favorites."

The woman introduced herself. She told her she was Mary Stevenson and shared a sixty-second version of her life story, including that she was a descendant of Robert Louis Stevenson and was once a dancer in the Follies.

"That may have been a while ago but I keep my tap talents fine-tuned, in case they're needed," she said, sounding a bit like Mae West.

With that, Mary did a little tap dance right then and there! Followed by a half curtsy and a wide smile!

Kathy clapped enthusiastically and

pointed to a chair, inviting her to sit.

Despite the difference in their ages, they spent the evening chatting and swapping stories about being in the entertainment business.

Just off the road from touring, Kathy mentioned how she had longed for a home-cooked meal "like my mom's, back in Ohio."

Mary's eyes lit up. She asked Kathy if she liked spaghetti.

Kathy nodded enthusiastically. Of course!

Well then, Mary would love to have her over for a nice, home-cooked spaghetti dinner!

Kathy was grateful, saying she couldn't wait.

A day or so later Kathy arrived at Mary's modest home in Buena Park. The front yard was filled with robust bushes and bright flowers, matching her host's colorful personality.

Mary opened the door and escorted her inside.

"What's up, kid? I hope you're hungry!"

Kathy nodded and breathed in the delicious aroma of marinara sauce wafting through the house.

She realized with a pang how much she

missed both her mom and her home cooking, both left behind in Ohio . . . a lot of miles ago.

Now nearly twenty-five, Kathy was primed for a little mothering from a kind soul on the road . . . and some good home cooking.

As Mary led her down the hallway to the kitchen, Kathy noticed lots of framed poetry on every wall. She stopped and read one.

"Mary, this is a beautiful poem!"

"You like it? I wrote it."

Kathy was impressed. "Really? You're good!"

"If you like that, there's a ton more where that came from!"

With a wink, Mary disappeared into another room, soon returning with a large cardboard box. She set it on the kitchen counter, turning it onto its side, causing hundreds of papers, large and small, some typed, some handwritten, to slide onto the countertop.

As Mary returned to the stove to stir her sauce, Kathy picked through and read a few poems.

"I love these," she murmured, thinking, *What are all these treasures doing in a cardboard box?*

Then Kathy noticed an old yellowed paper with a handwritten poem in pencil.

She lifted it up for a closer look and was surprised to see it was titled "Footprints in the Sand"!

"Mary, this is my favorite poem! My mother gave it to me . . . to remind me that, with God's help, I can weather any storm. It means the world to me."

Mary was still stirring the sauce on the stove. But the voice that came from her was decisive: "It means the world to me . . . to hear you say that."

Kathy looked up . . . at the back of her host. "Why? Are you a fan of it too?"

"A fan? No . . . I'm not a fan . . . I wrote it!" Now a little sadness could be detected in her voice.

"But it's . . . Author Unknown."

Kathy quickly reached for her purse, pulled out the wallet, and lifted the card out to show her.

Mary then turned, with a sweet smile.

"Well, nice to meet you then, Kathy," she said, adding with a little flair, "I . . . am Author Unknown!"

Filling the awkward silence, Mary promptly commanded, "Time to eat. Grab me a couple of those bowls from the table, will ya."

Soon they both sat down and began to

spin spaghetti on their forks, against tablespoons, and genuinely enjoyed the meal . . . "just like Mom's."

Kathy decided not to press Mary. Not to hit her up with a dozen questions about that famous poem. Just let her talk . . . when she felt like it . . . about that faded piece of yellow paper, in a tattered box.

After supper, Mary pushed back her chair and started talking . . . almost as if Kathy had just asked the question.

"I was fourteen when I wrote it," said Mary, looking above the window curtains at nothing in particular.

She told Kathy that she knew more about suffering than her young age might have suggested.

"There was extreme poverty during the Great Depression. Everyone we knew, in our area of Chester, Pennsylvania, faced terrible hardships. No money . . . no food."

Mary paused to take a sip from her cup of green tea.

"My mama died from tuberculosis when I was six. My older brother was killed in an accident a few years later."

Picking up the pace of her story, she went on to tell her attentive guest how one cold wintry day, she was feeling low. She had skipped school but found herself locked out of the house . . . and felt even lower. She plopped down on the porch steps.

"I prayed to God to give me something of value that I could give to others," she said. "Helping others always gave me a boost . . . a sense of purpose."

At that very moment, looking down, she said her eyes spotted something in the snow.

"Our cat had walked across the snow-covered front yard, leaving a trail of cat tracks."

Right then God began to help Mary form a new poem in her mind.

One night I dreamed . . .
I was walking in the snow with my
 Lord . . .

She paused.

No, that's not quite right, she thought. *It needs to be a warm place . . . where Jesus would walk in His bare feet.*

She started from the beginning . . .

One night I dreamed I was walking
along the beach with the Lord.

Soon the next line was coming to her.

Many scenes from my life . . . flashed
across the sky.
In each scene I noticed footprints in the
sand.
Sometimes there were two sets of
footprints.
Other times there was one set of
footprints.

Mary smiled at the memory of herself, a fourteen-year-old, realizing that God was weaving the words into her mind and her heart.

She continued:

This bothered me because I noticed
That during the low periods in my life
When I was suffering from anguish,
Sorrow, or defeat, I could see
Only one set of footprints.
So I said to the Lord,
"You promised me Lord that if I followed
You,
You would walk with me always.
But I've noticed that during the most
trying
Periods of my life there have only been
One set of prints in the sand.
Why, when I needed you most,
Have you not been there for me?"

A tiny smile appeared as Mary became wistful . . . Jesus was about to speak in her poem.

The Lord replied, "The times when you
 have seen
Only one set of footprints . . .
is when I carried you."

Kathy was crying.

It was like she was in an inner sanctum, where something beautiful and holy had been born. Yet it was so private that it was being saved just for her memory. It wasn't recorded, there were no pictures, and it was secretly being revealed in the humble home of a lovely lady who was telling her a story that only a handful of people on the whole planet even knew existed.

For a split second, she felt like she was intruding on a special relationship between this gentle lady and God, for, together they had intimately placed those words on that old yellowed piece of paper in the box . . . in pencil . . . when Mary's hand was that of a young girl . . . and her still unknown outcome was prodigy.

Mary told of how she shared the poem far and wide with friends, family, strangers, and people in need. And how a dancer she once knew said the poem had saved her life when times were hard.

During the Vietnam War, she said, she worked as a volunteer creating care packages — baking cookies — for our troops in Vietnam. And how she loved slipping a copy of her "Footprints in the Sand" poem into the boxes.

Yet Kathy remained in complete shock about its authorship.

"Why didn't you let everyone know that it was *you* who wrote one of the world's most inspirational poems?"

Mary answered with sadness.

"Because no one would believe me."

Kathy didn't hesitate.

"Well, I do! And I'm going to do something about it."

And she has. For all of her adult life Kathy Bee has helped Mary, in every way she could, to let people know who "Author Unknown" really was.

She got lawyers and forensic scientists involved, encouraged Mary to get a copyright on "Footprints in the Sand," and helped her with a book about her life story, letting the world know the truth: that Author Unknown is now KNOWN . . . and her name is Mary Stevenson.

POSTSCRIPT

That spaghetti dinner was the start of a very special friendship between Kathy and Mary.

Over the years, they collaborated, like Kathy writing the song "Momma Don't You Love Me" based on Mary's poem "The Little Seed."

In a newspaper article about the success of their song, Mary was noted as the author of "Footprints in the Sand" for the first time in print!

Kathy and Mary became close friends . . . sometimes like sisters . . . sometimes like mothers to each other . . . who were there for each other in good times and bad times.

When Mary was gravely ill, Kathy was there, sitting beside her friend . . . mothering her . . . and willing her out of a coma by playing music she knew would inspire her. And it worked!

They were friends to the end . . . and beyond.

REFLECTIONS

Is there a Mary or a Kathy in your life?

A surrogate mom who believes in you when the rest of the world doesn't?

Someone who is there for you when the

rest of the world isn't?

Isn't your life so much richer because of how they have guided your footsteps and strengthened your faith?

We should all be so blessed.

You walked through the waves;
You crossed the deep sea,
but Your footprints could not be seen.
— PSALM 77:19 (GNT)

3B
Louise — My Teacher Was a Second Mom

US senator John N. Kennedy spoke evenly in his drawl. "I cannot precisely tell you the names and order of the third, fourth, and fifth presidents of the United States . . . but . . ."

He paused and glanced around.

"I *can* tell you, in perfect order, the names of my third-, fourth-, and fifth-grade teachers."

Pretty much everyone knows Senator Kennedy was right. Teachers make a lasting and indelible impact on every one of us.

They often work for love, not money. They help children identify their purpose in life and prepare them for the future. They foster the leaders of tomorrow.

If someone asked you, right now, "Who was your most influential teacher?" how long would it take you to give the answer? Two? Maybe three seconds?

Louise's most influential and unforgettable teacher was Mrs. Bernice Bennett. She taught English and was the drama coach at Quincy High School.

It turned out she was also like a "second mother" . . . a person whom God places along your pathway in life to augment the value lessons and aspirations of your own mother.

"Mrs. Bennett demonstrated that she believed in me when I didn't believe in myself," Louise recalls. "She inspired me to follow my dreams and recognized that, despite my shyness, I had an innate passion to perform. So she nurtured it."

One day Mrs. Bennett told Louise that her ailing husband, a college professor, wanted to write his memoirs. However, he had lost the use of his hands due to a debilitating illness. She asked if she could hire Louise to come to her home after school to take dictation from her husband.

"I later realized that her primary motive was twofold," said Louise. "One, to give her husband encouragement; two, to give me a job that provided more access to her cheery and positive demeanor during our daily talks. In those afterschool chats, when I said, 'I can't,' she said I could. Her faith in me gave me faith in myself."

■ ■ ■ ■

"I know now that without her investing that time to gently coach me to step out, to shoot for the moon, I most likely would never have ended up in the entertainment industry and probably would never have reached the fulfillment of my childhood dreams," said Louise.

One of her most poignant memories of Mrs. Bennett came many years later. Louise had gotten her first Broadway show.

She recalls peeking through the curtain of the Lunt-Fontanne Theatre. "There she was, in the front row. Her presence was still encouraging, long after I'd graduated.

"But now I could see that my once dynamic and robust teacher was frail; she was struggling with her eyesight because of macular degeneration.

"I was flooded with emotions. It was her unselfish heart that brought me to this place. She's the one who saw something in me that I didn't see in myself and who helped me manage my shyness.

"I owe Mrs. Bennett a tremendous debt for what she did for me, and for so many other students, who looked up to her like a second mother. Her dedication helped us to achieve more than we could have ever dreamed or imagined!"

REFLECTIONS

What other profession has the potential to impact the lives of others in such a lasting, personal way?

Eighty-eight percent of American adults reported having a teacher who made a difference in their life.

In this unstable world, our children need wonderful educators and mentors like Bernice Bennett. Teachers are chosen by God to serve a greater purpose. They influence young minds and develop their abilities to positively contribute to the world.

So, whoever sets aside any command that seems unimportant . . . and teaches others to do the same . . . will be unimportant in the kingdom of heaven.

But whoever does and teaches what the commands say will be called great in the kingdom of heaven.

— MATTHEW 5:19 (GWT)

3C
Felisha —
Like a Mom to Me

You need to go check on her, thought Felisha Coyner as she passed the girl in the park.

A gracious woman with a warmth about her that encouraged others just by her mannerisms, Felisha enjoyed her four-block walk to and from work as a legal assistant in the US attorney's office in Charleston, West Virginia.

Not only did it help her achieve her daily "step count," but Felisha also enjoyed people-watching along the way.

"Hello," she would greet passersby in her gentle drawl.

But she never stopped to engage with anyone.

At least, not until that day.

She found herself drawn to a young woman, no older than twenty-three, with a little boy of about four. Felisha couldn't shake her unease.

Something's not quite right, she thought.

It tugged at her heart as the stride of her brisk walk broke, ever so slightly. Then she stopped.

Hesitantly, she turned and walked back toward the mother and child.

"Hey," said Felisha softly. "Are you okay?"

"I'm fine," said the girl, unconvincingly.

"Mind if I sit here for a minute?" Felisha ventured.

"No," she mumbled.

Felisha lowered herself to the curb.

The boy huddled behind his mother. When he dared to peek out, Felisha gave him a little wave.

What in the world are you doing? thought Felisha to herself. She had never done anything like this before and it felt, well, crazy.

But if something really was wrong, she couldn't live with herself if she didn't try to help.

"Your son is sweet," Felisha offered. "You must be a great mother."

The young woman just hung her head.

Felisha remained silent, allowing her space.

"My mother died a few months ago from cancer," the woman finally murmured. "I'm a loser with nobody to love me anymore."

Felisha looked at her with compassion. She wasn't speaking from self-pity. She wasn't saying "Poor me." She was experiencing profound sadness; deep and debilitating pain was pouring from her soul.

"You have a lot to be proud of," said Felisha, trying to comfort her. "You have this gorgeous little boy. Between the two of you, that's enough love for you both to get by."

The child peered out again, this time smiling shyly.

"It sounds like you looked up to your mom," guessed Felisha. "I'm sure your mom would want you to love yourself . . . so you can provide your son with as much love as your mom gave you."

The young woman slightly rocked her head up and down . . . as if she were agreeing . . . kind of.

There was a pause as the girl thought that over.

"I know you're right," she finally whispered. "I just feel . . . so lost . . . and lonely."

Felisha was already so far out of her comfort zone, what did it matter if she went a little further?

"Do you mind if I pray with you?" She was shocked hearing herself.

You see, Felisha didn't pray out loud. Ever.

She prayed faithfully and regularly, but never ever out loud with somebody else. Especially someone she didn't even know!

But the young woman said, "Thank you. That would be nice."

Inside, Felisha momentarily panicked.

Yikes! Now what do I say?

Still, she took both of the girl's hands into her own, opened her mouth, and words of prayer came tumbling out.

In truth, the prayer lasted only moments, but to Felisha it seemed like an eternity. An out-of-body experience. It was like she was looking down on herself, watching someone else praying.

When she finished, Felisha opened her eyes.

The young mother was bawling.

And the child had squeezed in between them. He was clutching Felisha's arms. Like he knew this nice lady was saving his mama.

"You're gonna be okay," said Felisha after a long while.

"You're gonna be okay."

"You don't understand," came the whispered reply. "I struggle with drugs. And even when she was sick, my mom kept trying to help me. I just wouldn't take her advice. I wouldn't let her take me to rehab or meetings. And since her death, I've been in a really dark place. I feel like I've let her down."

She patted her eyes and took a deep breath.

"I've been clean for two months. But I was just sitting here, getting ready to go get a hit."

Felisha was dumbfounded.

She was aware of how bad the drug problem was in West Virginia; kids died every day from relapsing. But nothing about this young woman gave away the depth of her inner strife. She was beautiful. Well-dressed. There was no earthly reason to guess she was in such trouble.

"In the past few weeks," the girl said, "I've been asking for a sign. A hint that my mother was still here with me. And in your prayer, you said the same thing she did. Literally. The exact same words she said to me."

She gazed deeply into Felisha's eyes.

"My mom just came to me through you and stopped me from getting high."

Felisha was completely undone.

Nothing like this had ever happened to her before.

With all her heart, she just wanted to scoop these two up and take them home with her.

But the girl's grandfather was coming to pick them up later and he'd worry if they weren't there.

So, before she went home, Felisha gave her phone number to the young woman.

"Please call me," she said. "If you ever need anything or want to talk, please just call."

Felisha never heard from the girl again.

In fact, she never even learned her name.

And when asked, Felisha still has absolutely no idea of anything she said in her prayer. Not a single word.

I wonder why God used me, she sometimes thinks, incredulously.

Why did God "wink" at her, the girl, and her son? Maybe because they needed help.

And maybe, just maybe, it was because Felisha was willing to step out of her comfort zone and give it.

Reflections

Felisha felt God nudging her to turn back and check on the young woman and her son.

Then two statements from the lips of the hope-starved girl remained in Felisha's memory long after:

"My mom just came to me through you

and stopped me from getting high . . ."

"I've been asking for a sign. A hint that my mother was still here with me. And in your prayer, you said the same thing she did."

When we step outside our comfort zone it can make us feel uncomfortable and even fearful . . . but that's when Godwinks happen.

Felisha was timid at first but she knew she had to be obedient to God's voice and speak to this mom and even pray for her.

One way to show that you love people is by simply asking if you can pray for them. The act of praying for somebody not only blesses them but blesses you.

The command Christ has given us is this:

> Whoever loves God must love others also.
>
> — 1 JOHN 4:21 (ESV)

4
Dog and Cat Moms

4A
Pam — Bullet Is My Baby

It was a quiet Mother's Day afternoon when the doorbell rang at Pam's home in Bellport, New York, on Long Island. She opened the door . . . and no one was there!

She closed the door and the doorbell rang again. She opened the door once more, this time looking down and noticing a basket . . . with a note attached: "Will You Be My New Mommy?"

Inside the basket was the cutest little fur ball of a golden retriever puppy she'd ever seen. He proudly wore a red ribbon around his neck and looked up at her.

For him, it was love at first sight . . . *Mama!*

For her, well, she burst into happy and sad tears. She had been going through a lot of hard times in the last year, and the pup was a parting gift – an act of kindness, actually — from an ex helping her through it.

■ ■ ■ ■

Bullet was a wiggly, happy ray of light who always seemed to be smiling. He was also very attuned to emotions — especially Pam's — and would be right there when her spirits needed lifting.

Bullet was her go-to cry pillow, constant companion, and best friend. He was such a great listener — she could tell him anything!

It was just the two of them for a pretty long time until she decided to reluctantly start dating again. Bullet was not impressed. He would hike up one side of his mouth in his best Elvis impersonation . . . and had one word for the male species: "Grrrrr."

That was . . . until he met Troy.

An air traffic controller, Troy worked temporarily as a security guard as a favor to help a friend — the manager of a hotel where Pam also worked.

There was a big snowstorm the night they met. Pam was working the late shift at the hotel's restaurant with her co-worker Marianne when Troy introduced himself. To make conversation, he asked what they were drinking.

Pam, who still considered all men "guilty

until proven innocent," answered flatly, "Hot chocolate."

Not deterred, Troy asked if he could get a hot chocolate. Pam pointed to an adjoining room.

"The kitchen's right there. You can get it yourself."

He headed to the kitchen and Marianne turned to Pam. "That was rude! He was just being nice."

Pam rolled her eyes and shrugged. *Whatever.*

When she left work an hour or so later, the snowstorm was in full effect. To her dismay, she found her car wouldn't start. When she went back inside, she was told to speak to the new security guard, Troy, about getting her car started.

When Pam sheepishly told Troy her problem, he pointed to the equipment room and said . . . with a smile . . . "That's the storage room. Jumper cables are there. You can get it yourself."

But . . . he did help her. And when her car wouldn't hold a charge, he drove her home in his truck after his shift ended.

Before leaving, he shoveled her driveway. She watched him from the front window, then offered to make him some hot coffee.

As they sat in the kitchen drinking their

coffee, Bullet — Pam's great protector — practically climbed into his lap. He even took Troy's boot and ran around the house with it.

Pam thought, *Bullet, you're a traitor! I don't know this guy yet!*

Troy quickly concluded that the way to Pam's heart was through Bullet.

At work, he dropped off a box of dog biscuits with hopes that she would agree to go out with him. One dinner led to another, and it didn't take long for her to see in Troy what Bullet had known instantly.

Pam and Troy Sica were married and started their life together with Bullet, who couldn't have been happier with the new arrangement. He was now the "furry" happy recipient of twice the fun, twice the treats, and twice the love!

When the couple snuggled on the couch, Bullet would lift their arms with his nose so he could get in between them — like *Hey guys, make some room for me, too!*

Pam and Troy wanted to start a family, but it turned out to be a long and painful journey. Pam suffered four miscarriages. And even though Troy and Bullet were there for her, every single time, the heartbreak was punishing.

With each loss, Bullet displayed an extraordinary sensitivity. Spending more time watching over Pam . . . snuggling with her.

"He's my baby," Pam would say. Bullet, by the look on his face, perhaps knew he was filling a huge void . . . left by the babies that Pam could not have.

After the last miscarriage, the doctor said solemnly, "Pam, I'm afraid you cannot have a child." That was heartbreaking.

Unfortunately, there was more heartbreak on the horizon.

Bullet seemed lethargic. He had no appetite.

Worried, Pam and Troy took him to see Dr. Laurence Cangro, his vet.

"Good boy," said Dr. Cangro, gently petting Bullet — one of his favorite patients for thirteen years.

The somber look on Dr. Cangro's face set off alarm bells in Pam's heart. She shared a concerned glance with Troy.

"Is Bullet going to be okay?" . . . her voice breaking . . . barely able to get the words out.

In Dr. Cangro's pause, she had her answer. She had fooled herself into thinking this day would never come.

“I’m afraid I don’t have good news. I don’t like the sound of his heart. And his enzyme levels are elevated. That’s an indication of liver cancer, which goldens are prone to get.”

Pam leaned against Troy, not sure her legs would support her. Then Dr. Cangro excused himself to go check on the ultrasound results, leaving them alone with Bullet.

Pam had always told everybody, *Bullet is my baby. I see into his soul, and he sees into mine.*

But now Bullet could barely keep his eyes open. He was drifting away, lying motionless on the cold stainless-steel exam table.

Taking his face into her hands, Pam leaned in and held his gaze, her brown eyes locking with his, willing him to stay awake and sharing a secret language they had spoken so many times before . . . *I love you! Always.*

Dr. Cangro returned. He spoke in a calm and measured way. “The ultrasound clearly shows that Bullet has a cancerous tumor on his liver. But we’re catching this early — there’s a chance we can save him. But there are things to consider. His age is a factor. He’s already exceeded the average age of goldens, which is twelve.

“And this surgery can be very expensive . . . about five thousand dollars."

Both Pam and Troy quietly sighed.

"I know. It's a lot. I want you to think about it overnight while we keep him comfortable here. You might want to pray. And talk it over with family and friends."

Dr. Cangro continued, "Bullet's getting up there. That doesn't mean he can't handle the surgery, and even live a couple more years, but it's a decision you should think about carefully."

Pam put her arms around Bullet, hugging him for a long moment. Then, swallowing tears, she whispered, "I love you Bullet . . . my baby . . . I'll see you in the morning."

The tears she had been holding back at the veterinary clinic flowed freely once they walked out the door . . . and they continued almost nonstop all the way home.

Finally, she managed to ask, in a cracked voice, "Troy, how can we possibly afford it?"

"We'll do what we need to do," he said supportively.

They spent the evening seeking the counsel of close friends and family. They talked to Pam's mother, her dad and stepmom in Florida, Troy's mom, and others.

Everyone knew the special relationship between Pam and Bullet and conveyed their great sympathy and sadness at the news. Yet, ever so gently, each raised the question of prudence — spending that kind of money on a dog who, if he even survived the surgery, had already exceeded the average life span of golden retrievers.

By the end of the night, Pam and Troy were exhausted, and just as confused as they had been before the calls.

Pam held her rosary tightly in her hand. It gave her some comfort. She looked up at Troy. "Even if we had the money, is it the right thing to do? I don't want him to suffer. He's my baby boy, my child, my shadow. Is it being selfish to want more time with him?"

Troy assured her it wasn't selfish. "We need to have faith. And trust that God will guide us to the right decision."

He held her close and heard her whimper softly until she fell asleep in his arms.

By the next morning, the answer wasn't any clearer.

They drove back to the vet, and in anticipation of Pam and Troy's return, Bullet was lying listlessly on an examining table. They asked for a few minutes alone with their furry friend.

Pam and Troy stood on opposite sides of the table. Pam laid her forehead against Bullet's as Troy put one hand on her shoulder and the other on Bullet's back.

Pam pulled her head back and again locked eyes with her canine soul mate.

"I know you're not feeling well, baby. But . . . we just don't know what to do. Do you want us to let you go?"

For a soundless minute, Pam looked deep, as deep as she could, into Bullet's eyes.

She then turned and faced Troy. No longer with a sad countenance. Now affirmative. "He's telling me . . . there's more for him to do."

Pam knew with divine certainty it wasn't time to let go. Someday it would be. But not now.

The surgery was scheduled and Troy figured out how they could borrow the money for the operation.

At Pam's request, a kindhearted veterinary technician sealed Pam's rosary in a sterile plastic bag so it could be near Bullet when he needed it most.

On top of that, the Sica family, plus friends and neighbors, were assigned to prayer duty.

Everything worked!

Dr. Cangro announced that with God's guidance — and a skilled surgical team — Bullet's operation was a success.

Bullet recovered in no time and was well enough to go on a road trip to Florida with Pam and Troy in early September. They would stay with Pam's father and step-mother during a week's vacation from Troy's air-traffic controller duties, coinciding with his birthday.

Bullet loved riding in the back seat, inhaling the different scents and breezes, all the way to Kissimmee.

Pam seemed to be feeling more tired after the long car ride but figured she would rest in the sunshine and read a book with Bullet at her side, and together they would restore their energy.

After a day or two, Pam's stepmother, keeping a watchful eye, boldly asked, "Are you sure you're not pregnant?"

Pam assured her she was not . . . with a puff of air dismissively passing through her lips.

The next time her stepmother was out, she picked up a pregnancy test for Pam, leaving it conspicuously on the sink in Pam and Troy's bathroom.

The next morning, Troy's birthday, Pam spotted the test in the bathroom, and thought, *What the heck . . .* and took it.

What? She was shocked! Her stepmom was right — SHE WAS PREGNANT!

Pam shook Troy awake and gave him the best birthday news ever — he was going to be a dad!

They came into the dining area, where Pam's father and stepmom were putting out toast, eggs, and bacon. Excitedly, Pam and Troy told them the news.

Bullet was excited too, and demonstrated just how much by tearing through the house with the empty pregnancy test box in his mouth!

It was a festive, gala few moments, until Pam's dad looked at the TV that had been playing in the background. "Oh no!" he shouted. "Look!"

The most joyful moments they could remember . . . instantly turned horrible.

They stood, like stone statues, watching the horror of that terrible morning in history . . . 9/11 . . . planes striking the World Trade Center.

Troy embraced Pam, now struggling with tears, "Oh good Lord . . . what kind of world am I bringing my baby into." She felt a familiar furry pressure against her legs. Bullet was at her side, once again trying to carry her sadness.

Troy tried to call his supervisor in the air-traffic control room at New York's Terminal Radar Approach Control (TRACON) to see if they needed him to rush back to work. He was advised that air traffic had been shut down indefinitely; that he could remain on leave until further notice.

Doctors treated Pam's pregnancy with kid gloves. Given her history with miscarriages, they kept a close eye on her.

Yet Pam felt cautiously optimistic. Maybe it was due to so many prayers being said for her — and by her — and Troy, but she felt this pregnancy would be different than all the others.

When she was in her third trimester, Pam's gynecologist advised that she was suffering from placenta previa, an abnormality that occurs in 1 of 200 births.

Her doctor prescribed bed rest and told her that placenta previa nearly always requires cesarean delivery.

When baby Troy was born in early April, about two weeks early, the birth was considered "complicated" and Pam was hospitalized for four days.

They were a little worried about how Bullet would react to Pam's absence, as well as being a new "big brother."

A nurse suggested giving Bullet one of the receiving blankets used to wrap baby Troy in the hospital. This way the dog would get familiar with the baby's scent. It worked like a charm!

Troy visited the hospital as often as he could, always reporting on Bullet's infatuation with his new blanket. "He carries it with him everywhere," laughed Troy, "even outdoors when he has to do his business."

Pam was thrilled when they told her she could take baby Troy home, even though he had some breathing difficulties. She couldn't wait to see Bullet's reaction to the new member of the family.

Bullet was the perfect big brother — protective, loyal, and loving. Wherever Troy Jr. was, that's where Bullet wanted to be. His favorite spot as a sentry was lying right under the baby bassinet, next to Pam and Troy's bed.

On the morning of Troy's first day back to work, nearly two weeks after the baby was home from the hospital, the alarm went off at 4:30 a.m. He turned it off and headed to the shower.

Pam heard Troy Jr. stir, so she got up and told Troy she was going to fix the baby a bottle.

In the kitchen, half-asleep, Pam was warming the bottle when she heard Bullet's nails tapping on the hallway floor as he raced from the bedroom to the kitchen.

"You wanna go out?"

She grabbed his collar and tried to escort him out the sliding glass doors, but he bucked and reared away from her.

"You don't want to go out?"

As if to urgently say "Follow me," Bullet ran back down the hallway toward the bedroom, barking loudly — he rarely barked — and then, at the door to the bedroom, he began barking and spinning in circles.

Pam had never seen Bullet act this way! Adrenaline coursed through her. She ran down the hall and into the bedroom, scooping up Troy Jr.

He was crying, but . . . there was no sound!

She took him into the light to see him better. In seconds, Troy Jr.'s face turned red, then purple, and then blue, before he passed out.

She screamed to Troy, "THE BABY'S NOT BREATHING!"

Troy, out of the shower and wrapped in a towel, assumed the baby was choking and tried clearing his airways, telling Pam to call 911.

She was already dialing.

"My baby's only nineteen days old, and he's not breathing!" she cried to the dispatcher.

The dispatcher assured her help was on its way and then gave her instructions, which she relayed to Troy.

In what seemed like about a minute, there was a banging on the front door.

How could that be? There was no siren, thought Pam.

It was a first responder.

But it was a Godwink. One of the EMTs on call lived four houses down. He had heard the 911 call come in and ran down the street with oxygen in hand!

Additional EMTs arrived minutes later.

Bullet seemed to transform from a dog to a wolf before Pam's eyes. He did not want these strangers near his baby. Pam put him in the kitchen, but he broke through the baby gate. She had to lock him in another room while EMTs worked to save the baby!

Baby Troy's breathing began again . . . thank God!

The initial first responder provided information to Pam and Troy — which hospital they were heading to, etc. — as they placed the child in the ambulance. He said only one parent could ride in the ambulance, which they suggested should be Troy, seeing he was dressed and ready to go. Then Pam could drive to the hospital on her own.

As the EMT was packing his gear, he looked at Pam and said thoughtfully, "You know, another few seconds and we would have lost your baby. Your dog is a hero."

Pam looked at him with a quivering lip, then said to herself, *Yes . . . Thank you, God . . . for Bullet . . . and for convincing us to save HIM!*

It suddenly sunk in. Those words she felt Bullet was communicating to her that day in the vet's office . . . *He's telling me . . . there's more for him to do.*

Baby Troy was in the hospital for two and a half weeks, diagnosed with double pneumonia, complicated by silent reflux and the discovery of two small holes in his heart.

During that time, Pam's rosary — the same one that was with Bullet during his surgery — was nearly always in her hands.

While other incubators had an assortment of religious pictures attached to them, taped to Troy Jr.'s incubator was a photo . . . of a smiling golden retriever . . . Bullet.

Troy's mom, Irene, stopped by the hospital a few times, so she had heard the story of Bullet's heroism, over and over. She got to thinking it was too good a story of hope for people not to know about it.

It just so happened that Irene had a friend at *Newsday,* one of metropolitan New York's most noted tabloids. She decided to call him the day Pam and Troy were finally taking Troy Jr. home for good.

Irene's friend at *Newsday* was so impressed with the story of Bullet that he went right to the editor's desk. Soon the gruff editor was going about assigning this upbeat story about a dog named Bullet that saved a baby, but not to one of the paper's well-known, seasoned reporters. Instead he yelled out, "Givens!" beckoning the paper's youngest, least experienced cub reporter.

Something needs to be said about the *Newsday* newsroom, representative of every New York City paper since September 11, 2001.

Just about every story for eight months had been about that tragic day.

A heavy cloud hung over the newsroom. The staff slogged their way through daily stories of horror, writing countless obituaries and reporting on heroic first responders in unthinkable circumstances.

The person who had to write the most heart-wrenching obits, talking to family after family, sometimes four, five, or six sad stories a day, was the lowest reporter on the ladder.

Now, like a newsroom version of Orphan Annie, twenty-eight-year-old Ann Givens was getting her marching orders from the editor, the one who serves as the quarterback of every newsroom.

He told her this was a quintessential Norman Rockwell story . . . a dog that saved the life of a baby in crisis. But it wasn't just any dog — it was a dog who himself had been saved earlier when the parents of the baby, against all reasonable advice, scraped up the money to perform a five-thousand-dollar operation on their fourteen-year-old dog.

"Think of this headline, Givens: 'Bullet Saves Baby' . . . maybe the first feel-good story since 9/11."

The next day Ann knocked it out of the park. Bullet and Baby Troy made the front page!

The internal story was headlined just as the editor imagined, while the banner headline on the tabloid cover — under Bullet and Baby Troy's photo — was "A LIFE-SAVING BULLET — Family Dog Alerts Mom to Baby in Distress, Just in Time."

Postscript

For his part, Bullet didn't care about his newfound fame. He was just overjoyed to have his "little brother" back.

Over the baby's first year, the two were quite a pair. Bullet would stand guard like a statue carved in stone beside the bathtub when Troy Jr. was getting a bath.

They often wore matching outfits — thanks to Mom Pam! When it was feeding time, one spoon from the baby food jar went to baby and another spoon from the dog bowl went to Bullet. The only time Bullet wasn't at Troy Jr.'s side was during diaper change — Bullet decided to excuse himself for that, thank you very much.

There was playful rivalry. Bullet would gingerly steal Troy Jr.'s pacifiers and bury them in the backyard! On other occasions he would eat the child's tiny socks. Never mind how Pam found out — we're not discussing that!

Bullet would sigh patiently when Troy Jr. used him like a hammock. The child thought nothing of draping himself over Bullet while the dog was lying on his back as Baby Troy took his time slugging down his bottle.

Like a cartoon dog, Bullet would freeze in place, shooting a look to Pam, like . . . *Help! I can't move, or he'll fall!*

Reflections

Maybe it's no coincidence that *God* and *dog* are spelled with the same three letters . . . or that *dog* is *God* spelled backward.

We often witness God using our furry four-legged friends as lifesaving angels on earth. And just like God, dogs provide us with comfort and unconditional love.

Bullet was like an angelic child for Pam, a companion for Troy, and for Troy Jr. a best friend and guardian angel.

Together Troy Jr. and Bullet celebrated their birthdays: Baby Troy's first and Bullet's sixteenth.

Six months later Bullet graduated to heaven. On that day, and every August anniversary since, a yellow butterfly has revisited the yard of the Sica home.

Three things will last forever
— faith, hope, and love —
and the greatest of these is love.
— Corinthians 13:13 (NLT)

4B
Cathleen — Gift-Wrapping Cats

Cathleen crouched down on the cold cement floor, careful not to startle any of the rescue animals in their cages. Some cats approached her cautiously, while others remained aloof, living up to their feline reputation for selective affection.

Newly single and recently relocated, Cathleen Cavin was a loving, fiercely protective single mother and woman of resilient faith.

That day, she was on a mission.

After a long and traumatic divorce, followed by a move to a small town just north of San Francisco, Cathleen wanted to give her four-year-old daughter, Cali, something special to help her adjust to the transition. Something new to love.

Frankly, after her own heartbreak and trauma, Cathleen thought she could use something like that too.

So, when the landlord of their condo

rental agreed to let them have a pet, mother and daughter went straight to the local animal shelter.

"Which one is ours, Mommy?" quizzed Cali, her eyes alight with excitement.

Cathleen let out a little sigh.

The cats were all cute, and there was a variety of colors, ages, and sizes to choose from. But none sparked a special connection that revealed they were "the one."

"Are there any others?" Cathleen asked the shelter worker.

Learning that the kittens were kept in back, Cathleen guided Cali to a small, cozy room where they found the fuzzy little fur balls wrestling playfully with each other, their tiny meows filling the air.

Cathleen couldn't help but smile. Yes, this is what she wanted.

"Look, Mommy, a heart!" cried Cali, drawing her mother's attention to two orange-and-white little twins, Butter and Ozzy.

Cali was right: the white fur of each kitten resembled half a heart, which, when they cuddled against each other, formed one whole heart.

Cathleen knew they had found "the one" — she just wasn't sure which brother it was, Butter or Ozzy.

Cali begged her mother to adopt both kittens, but Cathleen had to say no. Unfortunately, their landlord had approved only one pet. No more. On that he had been adamant.

So, after a half hour of deliberation, Cathleen and Cali left Butter at the shelter and brought home Ozzy.

But it wasn't the joyful experience of Cathleen's dreams.

Feeling lonely without his sibling, Ozzy cried incessantly.

After two weeks of his constant yowling, Cathleen made a decision. No matter what their landlord said, they were going back to get Butter and sneak him into their home.

So back they went to the shelter.

But their excitement vanished when they learned Butter was no longer available. Just two days before, a woman had adopted him.

Cali was tearful and inconsolable until Cathleen earnestly promised that someday, somehow, she would find Butter and reunite the twins.

But that night, Cathleen had difficulty sleeping. She chided herself for making her daughter a promise she knew she couldn't keep.

"God, I know I can't make good on that promise about Butter," she prayed. "Could you please help Cali forget I made it in the first place?"

Time passed. A couple of years. Ozzy adjusted and grew to love his new home as much as Cathleen and Cali did.

Finally, Cathleen, who had resisted every suggestion of every well-intentioned friend to start dating again, felt her heart had healed enough to give it a halfhearted try.

She took a chance and subscribed to an online dating service.

After one horrendous date in which a guy made Cathleen pay for both their meals . . . to another who drank six martinis before wanting her to climb on the back of his motorcycle for a ride . . . Cathleen was ready to give up.

But . . . she would give it one last try.

As she scrolled through the profiles, dismissing one guy after another, one picture caught her eye — that of a striking firefighter named Brian Herrera. A widower and single father. His kind eyes and confident gaze drew her to him, but it was the warmth of that smile that stirred an inner signal system.

Also, the photo he'd chosen for his profile was of him and his little girl, Ruby, on a camping trip. The way he described himself, his daughter, and his faith actually made

Cathleen's heart skip a beat.

She firmly swiped "yes."

First they started texting. But after a few days, Cathleen told Brian how much she hated texting. If he wanted to talk, please . . . just call.

He did. And they hit it off, talking for hours and hours; they had so much in common.

Both Cathleen and Brian were eager to meet face-to-face. But as two single parents, the juggling of their own schedules, as well as their busy little daughters', was like trying to gift-wrap water.

Eventually, both girls went out of town to visit their respective grandparents, and Brian suggested they meet for dinner at an Italian restaurant that happened to be Cathleen's favorite . . . a good sign.

When Cathleen walked in, Brian was already sitting in the booth where she and Cali always sat. Wow . . . now it was a Godwink sign.

Over dinner, they had flowing and easy conversation; then they decided to go dancing.

When it grew late, neither of them wanted the evening to end. So Brian tentatively asked Cathleen if she wanted to see his house, which was nearby, quickly assuring her his intentions were good.

By now Cathleen felt safe with Brian. So she accepted.

Brian's home was warm and cozy, filled with family photos and Ruby's colorful drawings on the refrigerator. Cathleen felt instantly at ease.

It was a warm night with a big full moon, so Brian suggested they retire to the backyard.

"It was so lovely," Cathleen later recalled. "Just hanging out, talking, and playing guitar."

After a while, Brian went to refresh their drinks.

He was in the kitchen, feeling happy and excited about the date, when all of a sudden he heard a scream. It was Cathleen!

"You stole my cat?!" she roared. "How did you steal my cat?!"

Brian raced to the backyard to find Cathleen, now standing, holding his cat and glaring at Brian with accusation.

"Who does that?!" she demanded. "What other surprises do you have for me?"

For his part, Brian was shocked and confused. What on earth could she be talking about?

He assured Cathleen that the orange-and-white cat was his and Ruby's. He quickly explained that before his wife died, she wanted to give Ruby a fond memory and something to remind her of her mother. So she'd gone down to the animal shelter and came back with . . .

"Butter?" asked Cathleen in shock and awe.

"How do you know his name?" Brian asked, equally shocked.

Cathleen told him the story of going to the shelter, seeing Butter and Ozzy — selecting the latter — and then making an unfulfillable promise to her daughter to one day reunite them.

Brian looked at Cathleen in total disbelief. Then he started laughing . . . infectiously igniting Cathleen in laughter too!

"This is wacky!" exclaimed Brian.

"Talk about fortuitous felines," giggled Cathleen.

Yet, remaining cautious, the next day Brian went to Cathleen's house to meet Ozzy for himself. But before either of them truly believed it, they compared adoption papers. Sure enough, it was true. They had been Godwinked by twin kittens.

Their very next date was with the girls, Cali and Ruby, who couldn't help but fall for each other, like BFF sisters, right away.

But that date also called for one more introduction . . . Butter and Ozzy!

Movies of the twin felines reuniting were like cartoon treasures. They snuggled, rolled around, and chased each other through the house to everyone's delight.

Then the best photo op of all. Cali, remembering what she saw that day at the pet shop, suggested they stage a photo with both parents, both girls, and Butter and Ozzy side by side . . . to re-create that image she once spotted of a heart in their fur.

There was only one thing left to do to complete a perfect family portrait.

Brian proposed. Cathleen accepted. And everyone said, "I do" (or "Meow, meow!").

POSTSCRIPT

Cathleen and Brian have been happily married for over a decade, while Cali and Ruby are real sisters and best friends. But none of this could have happened without the divine alignment of twin felines in their lives — may we say the most purr-fect Godwink ever!

Cathleen realizes that her prayer of long ago was answered . . . that time she was worried she'd made her daughter a promise she couldn't keep. To reunite Ozzy with Butter. True, she couldn't . . . but God could . . . and did.

And every Mother's Day the family has a special moment of prayer for Ruby's mom in heaven, for her critical role as a Godwink Link to bring the family together.

Reflections

If you look up *Godwink* in some dictionaries, you may see Cathleen and Brian's picture there! Just kidding — but you get the point.

> Godwink (n.) (god · wingk)
> An event or personal experience — often misidentified as coincidence — so astonishing that it is seen as a sign of hope from divine sources, especially when perceived as the answer to a prayer.

God can reveal a person's perfect mate through various methods. For Cathleen it was an "inner signal system" — probably the Holy Spirit that is noticeable within anyone who allows it.

You may feel that vetted internet dating services are helpful aids in your search for a potential partner. But never overlook the world's most efficacious dating tool, available free, to everyone everywhere: prayer.

Seeking guidance from God helps provide clarity and direction in your quest for a life partner if — yes, if — you sincerely pray and seek His will.

Look how God took all the difficult and broken pieces of Cathleen's and Brian's lives and divinely aligned them in exactly the right place at the right time — alongside two adorable kittens — so they could meet and fall in love.

He can do that for you too!

When the right place
Divinely aligns
With the right time —
Expect a Godwink.

— Squire and Louise
A Godwink Principle

5
Moms Divinely Aligned — Right Place, Right Time

5A
TunDe, Chris, and Mom — An Alignment of Kindness

It was a hot Friday night in September and the bleachers at the high school stadium in the small Georgia town were packed.

Everyone held their collective breath as their star quarterback, Chris Wright, took the snap, found his receiver in the end zone, and threw a bullet right into his hands.

Touchdown!

The crowd went wild, their cheers and feet-stomping testing the aluminum stands. There in the front row were his proud parents, Phil and Judy.

While no one was cheering more enthusiastically than Judy, her son's athletic achievements weren't what mattered most to her.

And it wasn't his great sense of style, which he inherited from her, of course, a beautician who always liked to look her best.

No, what she cared about was how he

treated people.

Every morning as he headed off to school, Judy said the same thing to him: "Be nice to someone today, Chris."

He expected that when he returned home, she would ask him what kindness he had shown that day, and he would have to deliver.

Even at a young age, TunDe Hector had a quick and bright smile.

She smiled even more brightly when her mother, Carolyn, brought home stacks of books for her. Carolyn was the part-time pastor of the local church and a full-time beautician with a ministry to make the world a more beautiful place, one person at a time.

In one of the stacks, TunDe found a slim green book of law. It was old and smelled faintly of moss, but TunDe, only twelve years old, loved it and read it cover to cover.

What stimulated her from those musty pages was the seed of a desire to be a lawyer. She tucked that evergreen wish into her heart.

A few years later, TunDe, who would soon be entering eleventh grade, noticed her father, Randy, was washing the car despite having a sprained wrist.

She stepped onto the porch and asked if she could help him.

He told her no, so she sat down on the steps and kept him company, watching as he repeatedly dipped the sponge into the sudsy water . . . squeezed it onto the roof . . . causing rivulets of dirty water to scurry down the sides of the car.

"What do you want to be when you grow up, TunDe?"

"A lawyer."

"A lawyer? You can do whatever you put your mind to, but I think you'd be a great nurse. I see your love and compassion for people — you care about everyone."

She thought about what he said.

Then she considered what her mother always taught her, that "love outweighs hate." She wondered, *Are they both pointing me in the same direction? A nursing career?* She wasn't sure.

A year later, her father was tragically killed.

As she dealt with heavy grief — and at the same time complications with college — TunDe was inspired by a kind neighbor who *was* a nurse. Her father's words returned to mind . . . and she put aside thoughts of being a lawyer. She decided to become a nurse.

Two decades later, it was a gray day as TunDe drove her silver Honda sedan down the highway in Athens, Georgia. The dreary overcast haze matched her mood. She hadn't found many reasons to smile lately.

She and her husband had separated a few weeks before, and times were tough. She worked hard as a home health care assistant. She had decided to give up on her nursing degree when her son was born, but she devoted herself to the difficult work of being a kind and caring nurse's aide while raising her family.

Her dad was right all those years ago. She loved everyone. And everyone loved TunDe. She had the cards and gifts from grateful families whose lives she had touched, to prove it.

Her son had spent the weekend with her in-laws and she was on her way to pick him up. She knew she had only five dollars in her wallet and her gas tank was nearly empty.

She hated to do it, but she planned to ask her mom for a few dollars to hold her over and buy gas before she got her paycheck in a couple of days.

Just then she heard the car's engine sputter and backfire.

OH NO!

She managed to steer the car onto the side of the highway and coast to a stop.

She was too tired and panicked for tears. Instead she prayed a desperate prayer.

Please help me, God! Please!

Chris Wright was heading to church, his wife beside him and his two daughters in the back seat of his metallic tan SUV. They were talking about their plans for the day when he noticed an abandoned silver Honda at the side of the road.

A mile before he took the exit for their church, he saw a woman walking alone on the berm carrying a gas can. He realized it must have been her car he had seen aways back.

His mother's lessons of kindness were part of his DNA.

Be nice to someone today, Chris.

He had never picked up a stranger before, but Chris felt God was placing a nudge right into his heart. He didn't even question it.

You must help this woman.

Chris dropped his wife and daughters off at the church and then circled back to find her.

■ ■ ■ ■

As TunDe walked along the exit with her empty gas can it began to rain. A light sprinkling. So light that she couldn't tell if what she was feeling on her face was raindrops . . . or tears.

Just then — divinely arranged and right on time — an SUV pulled up alongside TunDe. The driver leaned over to speak through the open passenger window.

"Do you need a ride?"

He was dressed in a salmon checkered button-down collared shirt, and he looked like a nice man. Even more than looks, she sensed he was a good person. In an instant, she trusted him.

"Yes."

TunDe climbed into his SUV, and Chris drove her to the closest gas station. They hit it off right away, making easy conversation about the situation.

Chris filled her gas can and drove her back to her car, deciding — with another heart-centered impulse — to give her whatever he had in his wallet. Forty dollars. He apologized and wished it were more.

TunDe was grateful for his gift. This meant she wouldn't have to ask her mother for money. As they went their separate ways, she smiled. His kindness to a stranger meant the world to her. She would never forget it.

Three years later, TunDe indeed had not forgotten.

She shared an inspirational Easter message at the church where her mother was the pastor. She told of the unusual blessings in her life, and how God had been there for her.

She recounted the story of how she had been stranded at the side of the road during a difficult time a few years before, and how a kind stranger gave her a ride, bought gas, and handed over all the money he had in his wallet.

A short while later, the phone rang before dawn, waking TunDe on her day off.

It was her manager. Apparently a coworker who had never called in sick in thirty years had finally done so. Could TunDe take her patients for her?

TunDe thought about all the things she planned to do on her day off, let out a sigh, and then of course said yes.

The timing of that change in plans would again prove to be divine.

One patient was Judy, a woman with

Parkinson's disease who was getting home hospice care. TunDe felt an instant connection with Judy and her husband, Phil.

Like TunDe's own mother, Judy had been a beautician. When TunDe arrived at their home, Phil was trying his best to fix his wife's hair because he knew it was important to her.

It tugged at TunDe's heart to see how hard he was trying. His love and devotion for his wife touched her deeply. She could tell he was nervous and upset . . . she wanted to do whatever she could to put him at ease.

She told him, "I know beauticians — my mother is one. They like to look good. I can help with that!"

TunDe gave Judy a bath and styled her hair. She selected a clean, matching pajama set for Judy and made sure she was comfortable in the recliner.

Then she asked Phil if it would be okay if she read some Bible passages to her. Phil gave her his enthusiastic blessing.

TunDe sat beside Judy, reading aloud messages of love and comfort.

Phil asked TunDe if she would be willing to work additional hours if they paid her directly. Although her life was busy with work, nursing school, and raising two sons, she agreed to do it.

Just then Phil's cell phone rang. It was his son. He stepped outside to talk.

Judy grabbed TunDe's hand and held it.

"Please don't go outside to talk. It makes me feel bad."

Judy knew something was wrong with her, but she didn't understand exactly what. She figured when someone went outside to talk, it was probably about her.

"I promise. I won't."

"Good."

Judy smiled and closed her eyes as TunDe held her hand and read her another passage.

Phil and Judy liked TunDe so much they wanted their son Chris to meet her.

The next evening, Chris came by from the gym, wearing workout clothes and a baseball cap. Always athletic and an advocate of exercise, he had found it also helped him manage the stress about his mom's illness.

Chris and TunDe stood at the island in the kitchen, getting to know each other.

Chris told her how much both of his parents loved her and wanted to hire her for as many additional hours as she had available. The whole family appreciated how she not only cared wonderfully for his mom's health needs and appearance, but also spiritually.

TunDe explained that she came by this ministry easily because her mother was both a beautician *and* a pastor . . . in Athens.

"I go to a church in Athens."

"Where?"

"Cornerstone."

"I met a nice man from that church once."

TunDe told him the story of being stranded at the side of the road when a man stopped, gave her a ride to get gas, and gave her all the money he had in his wallet. Forty dollars.

Chris's jaw dropped.

"TunDe, THAT WAS ME!"

They couldn't believe it! They were astonished they hadn't recognized each other but were blown away with how God had divinely aligned the paths of their lives . . . from their first encounter alongside a highway . . . to the bedside of Chris's mother.

On the Fourth of July, TunDe and Chris sat in the rocking chairs on the Wrights' porch and had a heart-to-heart talk.

They both knew the end was near for Judy. TunDe felt she needed to tell Chris something that was in her heart.

"I'm not sure how to say this . . . but the Lord spoke to me in prayer and told me

Miss Judy would be going home to be with Him on my birthday . . . July ninth."

Chris took in what she said and nodded.

"Thank you for telling me."

TunDe put a comforting hand on his shoulder.

"I'm sorry. I'm here for your family, whatever you all need."

Chris asked how TunDe had become a home health care worker. She was so exceptional at it.

TunDe told him about her father and his belief she would be a nurse. She had to quit nursing school to raise her family, but now she was going back and taking classes to become a registered nurse. With her years of experience as an aide, she was well on her way, but it still wasn't easy.

They both talked about the lessons of their mothers. Chris told how his mom sent him to school every day with a reminder . . . to show kindness to someone.

"That was a factor in my turning around to help you out that day along the road."

TunDe, wide eyed with God's wondrous divine alignment, exclaimed, "My mama, too! She always said, 'Showing someone love . . . outweighs hate.' "

Chris and TunDe looked at each other for a long moment, each marveling at how God was weaving their lives together . . . as they were looking on.

TunDe was right. Judy died on TunDe's birthday, July 9.

When TunDe got the message, she left her birthday celebration immediately and raced over to the home of Chris's parents to help out.

As he and his father planned his mother's celebration of life, Chris didn't think flowers would be what his mother would have wanted. He had an idea: to *really* honor his dear mother by inviting people to participate in a lasting act of kindness.

He thought of the kindness TunDe had shown Judy and her family and what TunDe had told him about nursing school.

He secretly set up an online charitable fund to raise money for TunDe's nursing school tuition. His goal was one thousand dollars. But after just a few days the goal was surpassed . . . by eight times!

Chris invited TunDe to stop by, saying they were sharing cake in honor of his mother . . . and hoped she could attend.

With his wife capturing the surprise on video, Chris began to express, on behalf of his mom, what TunDe had meant to their family in their time of great need. And how grateful they were.

The praise and appreciation made TunDe start to cry.

But Chris's presentation of a check for eight thousand dollars to cover nursing school expenses unleashed an avalanche of tears as TunDe thanked God and everyone who kindly contributed.

TunDe and Chris had no way of knowing that this was only the beginning. Life-changing blessings were on their way for both of them.

The heartfelt video of TunDe and the Wrights went viral with millions of views and before the charitable fund was closed, they had raised $37,000 for TunDe's schooling!

Their incredible story was picked up by many national news programs, and they were invited to appear on *Ellen, Dr. Oz,* and the Godwinks segment of NBC's *Today.*

POSTSCRIPT

With the money raised for her tuition, TunDe finished her nursing degree and later learned that her employer would cover tuition for further study at 100 percent.

But there was more: with TunDe's family

and the Wrights cheering her on, every step of the way, she was accepted into law school!

The dream to be a lawyer, carried in her heart since childhood, will culminate with a law degree just one year from the publication of this book.

And what kind of law will she practice?

In perfect alignment with her years of expertise in health care, TunDe will specialize in law that advocates for patients and home health care.

How divinely aligned is that?

Reflections

Chris received a tug in his heart that was the voice of God prompting him to turn around and help TunDe, who was walking by the side of the road.

When you are aligned with God, it enables Him to put you on a path of purpose. It not only opens up the door for you to receive His blessings . . . it enables you to bless others.

Learning to hear God's voice is key to being in alignment with Him.

That's when you begin to experience the joy of divine alignment, which nearly always leads to a Godwink.

When the right place divinely aligns with the right time . . . expect a Godwink!

— SQUIRE AND LOUISE
GODWINK PRINCIPLE #4

5B

JENNIFER, MARY, AND MOM — NICELY ALIGNED

Jennifer Bobbitt opened the oven door to check on the banana bread, filling her home with the most heavenly scent.

She took a long, deep breath — mmmm! It was her mother's recipe, a favorite comfort food. The bread only needed a few more minutes, which was perfect timing. Her friends — a close-knit circle of neighborhood moms — were about to arrive with their young kids for a playgroup.

Jennifer had looked forward to this gathering all week — they were moms helping moms . . . in good times or bad. And because they were all raising kids of similar ages, she came to appreciate her time with friends even more.

Recently Jennifer had revived her old childhood hobby of jewelry making. And her many friends immediately flooded her inbox with requests. Making jewelry was now not only keeping her busy, but it was turning into a small business.

The neighborhood moms arrived and the dining room table was soon covered with delicious desserts. As the women gathered, Jennifer noticed that her friend Brenda was running a little late, which was unlike her.

When Brenda arrived, Jennifer immediately knew something was wrong. Brenda tried to give them a reassuring smile, but her face showed concern and sadness. Trying to hold back tears, Brenda shared with them the tragic news about her good friend Mary.

"Mary's husband, Michael, just died, only months after being diagnosed with leukemia. My heart just breaks for them. Mary and Michael have three young children — ages eight, five, and the youngest is only two months old!"

Jennifer gave Brenda a comforting hug as the group reeled from this devastating news. They all had children about that age, and even though they had never met Mary, they could feel her pain intensely.

What would we do if something like that happened to us? Jennifer wondered.

Days passed and Jennifer couldn't stop thinking about Brenda's friend Mary and her great loss. She wanted to help in some way.

Then it came to her. Jennifer decided to make Mary a bracelet to let her know that many people were thinking of her and praying for her.

With a little sleuthing, Jennifer learned the birth stones for Mary, her late husband, Michael, and their three children. With loving care, she made Mary a beautiful bracelet to honor her family.

Jennifer gave the bracelet to Brenda and asked her to pass it on to her friend. She hoped that Mary would be comforted to know that people she had never even met cared about her and were praying for her family.

Yet little did Jennifer know that her act of kindness would be the first spark for wondrous Godwinks.

For Mary, the time surrounding Michael's death was a blur. He was her best friend, and their loving family meant everything to both of them. Now he was gone. And she was left to raise their children without him.

Mary loved the bracelet Jennifer made for her — especially the way it honored her family's strong bond, linking them all together right there on her wrist. She touched each bead with love.

To think a stranger would create such a touching and lasting remembrance is just amazing!

She was so moved by Jennifer's kindness, she wrote her a lovely thank-you note in beautiful penmanship.

After some time passed, Mary started attending a grief support group at her church.

At one of the meetings, she met a man named Russ who was grieving the loss of his wife and the mother of his children. She had died the same year as Michael, tragically killed in an accident during a family vacation.

As they shared their grief, the friendship between Mary and Russ grew. His children were away at college, and he was lonely. She had her hands full, raising three young children on her own.

Their grief brought them closer. No one else could really know what they were going through, and it was a real blessing to spend time with someone who understood the other's heartache so completely.

As they moved along their difficult journeys of loss, their paths overlapped more and more, and their friendship deepened into love.

When Mary and Russ decided to get married, Mary knew she wanted to wear Jennifer's beautiful bracelet — representing her whole family — on her wedding day.

Over the many months, the two women had never met.

So, Mary called up Jennifer to tell her the good news — and to ask if she could add another gem to the bracelet to represent Russ joining her family in such a way that would honor both men in a meaningful way.

Jennifer was thrilled about Mary's newfound happiness and felt honored to fulfill her request.

She thought long and hard about it and then redesigned the bracelet to move Michael's stone to the center . . . along with the three for the children. Near the clasp would be the crystals for Mary and Russ, side by side.

The bracelet now told a story — of love, loss, and renewal — a perfect reflection of Mary's journey.

When the redesigned bracelet was ready, Jennifer wrapped it, wrote a note to Mary, and placed it in a bag with a Godwinks book she had just finished reading. She then placed it on Mary's doorknob.

Still, the two had never met!

Later that day, Mary called to tell Jennifer how much she loved her "new" bracelet and the way her redesign honored one man and celebrated another. She asked how much she owed her.

Jennifer answered, "Nothing. I was happy to help. Just please gift it forward someday."

A year later, on a cold Saturday in January, Mary and her twelve-year-old daughter, Molly, stopped at the grocery store. As Mary parked her car, she told Molly they only needed a few items for dinner, and that it shouldn't take long.

They couldn't help but shiver and quicken their pace as they hurried across the windy parking lot.

As they approached the store's front entrance, they were shocked to see an older woman lying on the ground and bleeding terribly. She had fallen hard on the pavement and hit her head; her glasses were broken beside her and she appeared to be in a lot of pain.

Her distraught husband was trying to make a call to his daughter for help on his cell phone.

Repeatedly he asked his wife, "Honey, what's her number, what's her number?!"

Mary assessed the situation and asked if anyone had called 911.

Someone had and they were on the way.

Several people stood around, unsure what to do and afraid to move or touch the injured woman.

So Mary stepped forward to comfort her and then realized that she must be getting really cold on the ground.

Firmly, Mary asked her daughter to run to the car to get the blanket in the back seat. Molly ran off and quickly returned.

Carefully placing the blanket over the woman, Mary assured her — and her husband, who was understandably rattled — that everything would be okay. Help was on the way and she and Molly would wait until the ambulance arrived.

Mary was moved by the man's love and concern for his wife. She worried about him too, calculating that he would probably go in the ambulance with his wife, leaving their car behind.

Since he was having trouble connecting to his daughter by phone, Mary wondered if he had anyone locally who could help.

She promptly wrote her own name and

number on a piece of paper, while telling both of them that if they needed anything, like a ride home from the hospital or back there to the grocery store to pick up his car, to be sure to call her. She'd be happy to help!

"What's your name?" asked Mary.

"Linda," said the woman, feeling better now.

The next day, Linda was out of surgery and resting in her hospital room with two steel rods fusing her broken arm. Her husband, Jim, much calmer now, was sitting beside her.

Trying to erase the fear, pain, and embarrassment of her fall outside the grocery store, Linda was excitedly repeating the story of her "angel in the parking lot" to her daughter Jennifer, who had by now rushed to her mother's side.

Linda continued her story, telling how the woman sent her young daughter for a blanket to keep her warm . . . and offered rides anywhere they needed to go.

"Did you get her name?" asked Jennifer, thinking that she would love to call and thank this wonderful person. "She *sounds* like an angel!" she added.

Jim fished in his pocket for the slip of

paper the lady had given him. He handed it to his daughter.

Jennifer took it and stared at it . . . speechless.

She recognized the handwriting. She recognized the name. She couldn't believe her eyes.

Both Mary and Molly were worried about the woman in the parking lot.

Mary hadn't heard from the woman's husband, so she had no way of knowing how that dear lady was faring.

She and Molly had just been praying for her when the phone rang.

"Is this Mary McNamara?" a voice asked.

"Yes, I'm Mary."

"Well, you're never going to believe this, but this is Jennifer Bobbitt. I made the bracelet for you. Do you remember when you asked me how much it cost, and I said, 'Just gift it forward'?"

"Yes."

"Well, you really did, Mary! That woman you took care of in the parking lot . . . WAS MY MOTHER, Linda!"

"Your mother? No way!"

Mary and Jennifer, both incredulous, laughed with delight!

They marveled at how their lives had intersected in such a powerful, meaningful way, a true Godwink, reminding them that even in the most challenging times God brings people into our lives at just the right moment.

Their story wasn't just about a bracelet. It was about the unseen threads that connect each of us . . . weaving a tapestry of kindness, love, and support. It was a reminder that even small acts of compassion can have a profound impact, creating ripples that bring people together in ways that only God can orchestrate.

Now, you might ask, did Jennifer and Mary ever meet? Yes, months later — and quite fittingly it was just after Mother's Day.

Reflections

It doesn't take a lot to be an earth angel in someone's life.

- Baking banana bread with love . . . and sharing it with an encouraging note
- Being there for a mom going through the challenges of raising kids
- Or maybe, like Jennifer and Mary . . . crafting a bracelet with care and giving

it freely to a stranger who has suffered loss
- Providing a blanket to warm and comfort a woman who is injured and cold
- Offering a ride to a husband who is concerned for his wife's well-being

Neighbors helping neighbors. Strangers helping strangers. Moms helping moms.

It's letting God use your hands and heart to make the world a better place. Not for any reward, but because it is the right thing to do. Because it's what He called you to do.

When a wonderful Godwink occurs while you're doing for others, like when a stranger you prayed and cared for turns out to be the very person who prays and cares for someone you love the most, like your own mother, that's God winking at you! He's showing He's pleased.

> Do not forget to do good and to share with others,
> for with such sacrifices, God is pleased.
> — HEBREWS 13:16 (NIV)

6
Cherishing Holidays with Mom

6A
Louise — Mom's Christmas Pizzelles

Life has given me some amazing blessings.

At the top of the list would be my mom, Grace. Even though she was small in stature — four feet eleven — she stood tall in the eyes of her children and grandchildren.

If I had one word to describe Mom, it would be *spitfire.* The grandkids lovingly called her "the Energizer granny." She was as vibrant and sharp as could be, even at the birthday party celebrating her arrival at one century old.

We dreaded the day when we would no longer hear her voice, her laugh, and her wise words. That sad day arrived when Granny turned 101 and graduated to her heavenly home.

As we approached the Christmas season that year, I remembered, as a little girl, when Mom allowed me to make pizzelles next to her for the first time. I was so excited as the old pizzelle maker turned out those thin crunchy four-inch waffles.

My job was to shake white powdered sugar over each waffle while it was still hot. The white powder was spattered all over my face, hands, and clothes. And you should have seen my dog Spotty! She looked more like Casper the Ghost. I wish I had a picture of that memory!

My youngest son, Danny, who lived two thousand miles away, was facing personal challenges and having a difficult time about Christmas. He was crushed that he was going to miss being with the family. That year in particular.

His mind was filled with memories of gatherings at Granny's house, sitting around the dining room table where we laughed, told stories, and gobbled up tons of food. Then, of course, nibbled on Granny's pizzelles.

I was thankful that I would be spending that Christmas with my stepdaughters Robin and Hilary. Sadly, they had also recently lost their mom. So I was sure we'd be shedding tears together, along with miles of smiles for humorous times remembered.

Robin had a great idea. For the first Christmas without her mom, she decided to make one of her mother's favorite recipes, apple pie.

As Robin pulled out the Crisco-stained card from her mom's recipe box, she felt a warm connection. With every ingredient mixed into the bowl, she thanked God for the gift of love from her mom's apple pie.

I thought I would follow Robin's wonderful example. So, shortly before Christmas, I went down to the basement and lugged up Granny's well-worn pizzelle maker, determined to make Granny's favorite recipe.

At about the same time, every phone call with Danny left me with the feeling that he was trying to hide his melancholy about Granny and not being home for Christmas.

I had an idea. Ship him his box of gifts with a cookie tin placed at the bottom.

When Danny opened it, he read the note and couldn't help but smile through his sadness.

It said:

Dear Danny, this is the first time your mom has ever made these Christmas pizzelles without Granny at my side.

I found her original recipe; written by Granny's hand in faded pencil.

So, this year I've teamed up with the Spirit of Granny to take you back to Christmases past.

And . . . I'm laughing now . . . imagining you and your dogs doused in powdered sugar with every bite of these delicious pizzelles.

Danny reported that Granny's pizzelles warmed his heart for the holidays.

Now our family has a new tradition: serving our mother's treats to everyone gathered around the table, along with a couple of anecdotes about our moms, written on cards and read by our grandchildren.

That's about as close as we can get to having the motherly hugs that go with those wonderful recipes.

Reflections

If you are struggling with grief, thank God for holidays past, perhaps those times when a lost loved one helped you start a new tradition of sweet memories.

And pray for the gift of Godwinks!

Every Godwink is a tangible connection to an unseen God.

Every good and perfect gift is from above,
coming down from the Father of the
heavenly lights. . . .

— James 1:17 (NIV)

6B
Elaine and Avery — Elfie and the Snow Globe

The air was crisp and cool — well, as cool as it gets in Dallas in December — when Elaine Hargrove stepped onto her daughter's elementary school playground as a volunteer recess helper.

A compassionate woman with a gentle southern drawl and infectious smile, Elaine had a way of making everyone she came in contact with feel instantly welcome and at ease.

She drew a deep breath and smiled.

Soon enough the buzzer would blare, doors would burst open, and a flock of laughing, chattering children would scatter over the playground.

But for now, the sky was clear, the sun was bright, and all was deliciously quiet.

Elaine treasured little moments like these, especially in the hustle and bustle of a busy Christmas season.

■ ■ ■ ■

Elaine and her family loved Christmas. Everything about it. The decorations. The food. The presents. The warmth and fun of family and friends. But as Christians, they most loved celebrating the birth of Jesus and His example of loving and giving.

Yet, as Elaine was well aware, Christmas didn't bring out the same warm and fuzzy feelings for everyone. In fact, a few nights ago while tucking in Avery, her six-going-on-twelve-year-old daughter, mentioned Jada, a new classmate.

"She doesn't have any friends, Mommy," Elaine remembered Avery saying sadly. "She sits by herself." Then she added, "I asked her if she wanted to swing, but I think she was shy."

Elaine gazed at her daughter with pride. Not only for her caring heart but especially for her efforts to befriend Jada by inviting her to play.

Now, in the peace of the playground, Elaine was reminded how they had said a short prayer, asking God to reveal any ways Avery could show love and care to her new classmate.

The bell signaling the start of recess sounded loudly.

Elaine readied herself.

A second later, an army of elementary-age children exploded from the school for recess. Some kids brought a soccer ball and started a game. Others played on the monkey bars and swings.

Then Elaine saw her. A little girl matching Avery's description of Jada as she took a seat, alone, on the brightly painted Buddy Bench.

Also called a friendship bench, a Buddy Bench is a designated place in a schoolyard or park where children can go if they are feeling isolated or lonely. When they sit there, it signals to others that they need someone to play with or talk to.

What a wonderful addition to the playground, thought Elaine. *There should be Buddy Benches all over the city for anyone of any age who needs a friend!*

She quietly approached the little girl.

"Hi," she ventured. "I'm a parent volunteer. Is it okay if I sit here with you?"

The child barely looked up as she nodded.

Elaine waited another moment. "I'm Elaine," she said, gently. "What's your name?"

"Jada," came the weak reply.

"What brings you to the Buddy Bench today, Jada?"

Jada was quiet.

Elaine waited patiently.

"I miss my mom," Jada finally whispered.

Elaine was not surprised. Earlier that morning she discussed Avery's concerns about Jada with her teacher.

"One of the teachers told me you moved here with your dad . . . but your mom still lives in another state . . . Is that right?"

Jada nodded.

"So, you don't get to see her as much as you'd like?"

Then the child looked directly at Elaine for the first time. Tears welled in her eyes and trickled down her little cheeks.

"All I want for Christmas is to see my mommy," she said.

Elaine could hardly hold back her own tears that were straining to get out! *Oh, this poor sweet girl.*

They talked for a while, with Elaine trying to soothe the child as best she could, but never feeling as if anything she said or did was helping.

It was gut-wrenching.

Then the bell rang and Jada stood up, gathered her emotions, and blended into the flow of children returning to the building.

That night at home, Elaine decided to use this as a teaching moment for Avery. So, when dinner, homework, and dishes were done, Elaine sat down with her daughter on the sofa, in the glow of their twinkling Christmas tree lights, and shared what Jada had said that day at school.

After a brief explanation of their conversation, Elaine discussed what it meant to have compassion for what others are going through, especially during the holidays. How even though Christmas was about fun and Santa and receiving presents, it was, more importantly, about Jesus, family, and doing sweet things for other people.

Suddenly, Avery's eyes lit up with revelation.

"I know what to do, Mom!" she said as she raced to the mantel, where the family's stockings were hung, and where Avery's adored "Elfie" — her Elf on a Shelf — sat guarding the living room.

Elaine watched in curious delight as Avery whispered into Elfie's ear, knowing Avery loved Elfie even more than Santa.

When she was finished, she returned, wearing a proud smile.

"It's fixed, Mom," said Avery. "I asked Elfie to bring Jada a snow globe with a place in it for a photo. That way she can put a picture of her mom in there. And when she shakes it up, it will be like snow falling and having Christmas with her mom."

Elaine choked up! She was flabbergasted at not only her child's kind heart, but at how God can work through the willing vessel of a six-year-old.

Yet as sweet as Avery's request was, it also seemed highly challenging. Elaine wasn't sure if such a snow globe even existed. She had never seen one with a slot for a photograph.

Maybe I can find something on the internet tomorrow. After all, Avery still believed Elfie could do anything, so Elaine needed to make it happen. But first . . .

"Tell you what," said Elaine, reaching for Avery's hand, "let's pray and ask God to help Elfie in his mission."

The next morning, just as Elaine opened her computer to see what she could find online, the doorbell rang.

Cheryl, her mother-in-law, was at the door carrying a big bag of "treasures."

Over coffee, Cheryl explained how she had been helping her own mother clean out her closets. She decided some things were too good to throw away, so she brought them over to see if there was anything Elaine and her family might be able to use.

And what was the first thing she pulled out of the bag?

Believe it or not, it was a brand-new snow globe, still in its box, with a slot in it . . . in which to place a photo!

Exactly what Avery asked Elfie for!

Elaine was amazed!

The next day at school, Avery gave sweet Jada her best Christmas gift ever!

And for Avery, Jada, and Elaine . . . it was one of their best Godwinks ever!

Reflections

This story shows us how important it is to have childlike faith.

Elaine and Avery's very specific prayer to "help Elfie" locate not just a snow globe but one in which a picture of her little friend's mother could be inserted left no room for doubt in Avery's tender heart.

Without knowing if such a snow globe had even been invented, she appealed to God in a simple and matter-of-fact way.

He responded with a simple Godwink.

Kids have active imaginations and a wonderful capacity to believe without question.

Oh, to have the faith of a child. Isn't that what God is looking for in all of us?

> I tell you the truth, unless you turn from your sins and become like little children, you will never get into the Kingdom of Heaven.
>
> — MATTHEW 18:3 (NLT)

6C
Carol — Best Home-Alone Thanksgiving

Thanksgiving had always been a special time for Carol's mom, Mary Anne. The heaping plates of food. The laughs. The stories at the dinner table. The family had spent countless hours in her mom's kitchen making the food in preparation for the day.

Yet that felt like a lifetime ago. Dad had passed away. Mom was now eighty-eight, living by herself in St. Louis. And the rest of the family was scattered across the continental US — from Washington State to Florida to New Jersey. The closest was Carol's sister, Debbie, who lived four hours away.

Still, the family always managed to tag-team and pull together as many as possible, to be sure that Mom had company for the holidays.

This year plans were set . . . but collapsed at the last minute. Everybody who was coming got sick, leaving Mom with the prospect of being home alone for Thanksgiving. And the freezer was empty!

Mary Anne, being the understanding mom she'd always been, reassured the family that she would be fine, but Carol could hear the disappointment in her voice.

This left the family scrambling. It seemed like an impossible predicament. It was Thanksgiving Day, and for the first time ever, Mom wasn't even going to have food. Carol's heart was breaking. She prayed, *Lord, please make a way.*

Across the country in Seattle, Joey, Carol's youngest son, couldn't believe his ears as his mother broke the news to him. Grandma was not only alone for the holiday, but without a special Thanksgiving meal?

He had always been very close to his grandmother and was determined to resolve this problem. But how? It was already Thanksgiving morning. How many restaurants would be open in St. Louis?

Then it hit him. It seemed like a long shot. But he recalled his grandmother talking about her favorite restaurant — a pit barbecue place not far from where she lived.

He quickly searched for the number.

Hoping against all odds, he dialed. It rang. Joey waited. It rang again. Still no answer.

His heart began to sink. Maybe it was too late. With each ring of the phone, his heart fought against hopelessness. *God, make a way,* he thought.

"Hello, Honey Pit Smokehouse," a voice answered.

Joey couldn't believe someone had answered.

"Are you guys open today?" Joey asked.

"No, I'm sorry. We're closed for the holiday."

The man, who incidentally was named Joe, explained that he had just popped by the restaurant for a moment when the phone rang.

Joey let out a sigh of disappointment.

The man on the other end of the phone call could sense how troubled Joey was.

"What was on your mind?"

Joey explained that due to unfortunate circumstances, his grandmother was alone for the holiday, and he wanted to find a way to make it special. He had hoped to order food from her favorite restaurant.

"But, darn, you're closed," he ended.

"I see . . . ," the man said.

He paused a moment. "Let me see what I can do. Can I call you back?"

Joey agreed and waited by the phone. It seemed like an eternity, but finally Joe called back. With a plan.

An hour later, Mary Anne was sitting in her living room when the doorbell rang. She wasn't expecting company. Peering through the side window, Mary Anne saw a man standing patiently outside, a small child in one arm and a bag in the other.

Opening the door, the bold smell of turkey and fixings came flooding in.

With a big smile he said, "Joey and your family wanted you to be sure you had something special for Thanksgiving."

She could hardly believe it.

Not only that, but he took a photo with Mary Anne and his little baby, promising to text it to Joey as confirmation of the successful surprise visit!

Later as Mary Anne and Joey shared the story with the family over the phone, Carol could hardly keep from tearing up.

God had done the miraculous. From giving Joey the idea to reach out to a kind stranger, who went home and boxed up turkey, mashed potatoes, and gravy from his own family's meal so that Mary Anne would have a special Thanksgiving meal from her favorite restaurant chef — God had also winked at Carol's whole family, as if to say, "I am faithful."

REFLECTIONS

No matter what is going on in your life, God's steadfast love for you will never, ever end.

Every day He has a brand-new supply of mercy and grace.

In Mary Anne's case, a brand-new supply of food for Thanksgiving dinner!

Grandparents play an important role in our lives. They are at the heart of so many of our favorite memories. They often tell us stories of their own struggles and how they learned to appreciate the simple things in life.

The lessons we learn from our grandparents play a huge role in shaping our past, present, and future.

Grandparents don't ask for much but they do appreciate a little pampering now and then. The smallest of things can bring them a lot of happiness.

Today, let's thank God for the grandparents we have and do all we can to bring them a little joy.

Even when your hair is gray I will carry you;
I have done this, and I will lift you up,

I will carry you to safety.
— ISAIAH 45:4 (NAB)

6D
Darla — First Christmas Without Mom

The town streets were adorned with festive Christmas lights, wreaths, and decorations. In front of the strip of shops that line Main Street were the soldiers collecting toys for children and the local Salvation Army Santa ringing his bell.

Darla sat in her car looking out at the whimsical scene before her. She thought about the years she had spent coming to downtown with her mom. They had found so many fun gifts in the eclectic shops.

This would be the first Christmas without Mom, and Darla couldn't help but feel the deep sadness of never being able to have this little annual adventure with her again; never being able to hear her voice or chat with her.

It hadn't been that long since her mom passed. And it caught the whole family off guard, especially her dad. Most days she felt as "okay" as one might expect, but the holidays were bringing all those feelings of loss and sadness flooding back.

The main thing that brought the family comfort was her sister-in-law Phyllis's dream about Mom going to heaven. She told them that Darla's mom said to tell the family that she was happy, she was home, and "All that matters is Jesus — and what we do for Jesus."

Now, sitting in the quiet of the car, Darla could hear those very words spoken — in her mom's own sweet voice — as she had said them so many times through the years.

The emotion of spending Christmas without Mom draped over Darla like a heavy quilt. She pressed her lips as tears of deep sadness filled her eyes.

After a few moments, she gathered herself and exited the car. The chill of the cool December air caused her to sink tightly into her overcoat as she made her way across the street to the row of shops.

Entering into a little Christian bookstore, she was greeted with the chime of the bell that let the shopkeeper know a customer had entered. The room swirled with the aromas of cinnamon, sugar cookies, and fresh pine.

She wandered through the displays of the

latest books on prayer, Bible study resources, and bestselling Christian novels, finding her way to the holiday whatnots and decorations.

She wished Mom could be there with her. She would love all the trinkets and Christmas-themed wall art.

As she walked to the ornaments, she smiled at the thought of how much her mom loved every ornament they'd gotten over the years. But then she had to shake off the thought . . . *Am I going to make it through this first Christmas . . . said to be the toughest?*

Darla firmly began to walk back to the front . . . to go find another store . . . when a strange but warm sensation tugged at her. She felt her attention drawn to the shelf next to her.

Looking up on the top shelf, she saw an ornament sitting alone — turned sideways, making it difficult to see what it was.

She reached up and took it in her hand. Pulling it down, she nearly dropped it when she saw what it was.

It was an ornament with words etched on it:

WHEN YOU GET DOWN TO IT,

She was covered in goose bumps looking at those words.

She thought about all the people who had come into this shop . . . who had passed by that ornament.

Yet it seemed that God and her mom had come up with this perfect little message — at the right time and right place — to speak to Darla's heart. God was winking at her.

He had hidden this gift away on that shelf, just waiting for Darla to discover it.

Darla's mom had always told the family that Jesus was "the reason for the season." Now, every year, when the tree goes up for the holiday and Darla hangs that ornament, all of the memories of her dear mother come flooding back.

But no memory exceeds the importance of Mom saying, "All that matters is Jesus — and what we do for Jesus."

REFLECTIONS

Amid all the fun, the food, and the family, it's easy to miss Christ in Christmas.

Darla's mom taught her that she needed to slow down and reflect on the true meaning of the season.

■ ■ ■ ■

If you find yourself busy and overwhelmed because there are so many things to do, take five: sit down, say a prayer, and enjoy the presence and love of our Savior.

His birthday gives us hope and a future.

> I am leaving you with a gift — peace of mind and heart.
> And the peace I give is a gift the world cannot give.
> So don't be troubled or afraid.
> — JOHN 14:27 (NLT)

7
Moms and Daughters — A Special Bond

7A
Kristine — Mom's Lost Crucifix

Early one morning, Kristine DeCarles left home to walk the short block to her family's business, Stock's Bakery, a one-hundred-year-old staple in Philadelphia founded by her great-grandfather.

A bighearted woman of tenacious faith, deep family, and community connection, with a laugh so hearty it explodes with a zest for life, Kristine loved this time of day.

The air was crisp and cool. The sky was awash in a palette of pastels. In the calm before the chaos of a busy workday, she could almost feel God walking alongside her.

So much of Kristine's life had taken place on this single block. Three of its charming row houses had been owned by various family members over the years, including her current residence and her old childhood home.

As always, Kristine was flooded with

memories as she walked past each home. What fun it had been, growing up with so many cousins, aunts, and uncles nearby, living in each other's pockets.

The bakery was a rewarding but demanding business, requiring early-morning baking and late-night bookkeeping. So it became a family tradition that whoever was in charge of the business lived rent-free in one of the houses.

Kristine smiled, thinking of how running the business never tempted her mother, Bernice.

When Kristine was eight she remembers her grandfather deciding to turn the business over to her mother and father; Bernice would run the store while Karl ran production.

Yet, in her heart, Kristine's mom felt she needed to place 100 percent of her focus on raising the family.

As a result, her dad stepped up and successfully took on running all aspects of the business for nearly fifty years.

Meanwhile, her mom lived her dream, birthing four children in five years and embracing motherhood.

We had such a great life growing up, thought Kristine, gratefully.

She was the youngest daughter and shared an especially close bond with her mom. While Karl and the other children were logical and analytical, Kristine and Bernice were right-brained, nurturing creative types. But make no mistake about it, all of Bernice's kids were taught to believe in the power of prayer.

A devout Catholic to whom faith was paramount, Kristine's mother kept a small wooden crucifix next to the bed to remind her of God's love and presence and the need to pray. Just three inches tall, it balanced on a little display base her mom kept on the bedside table for as long as Kristine could remember.

But strangely, that little wooden crucifix became lost. Bernice fretted about not being able to locate it

Then, when Kristine's mom had heart issues, couldn't climb the stairs, and needed to sell their home in favor of a single-level bungalow they owned in New Jersey, Kristine remembered her mother's panic. And how the family spent one whole day looking for the lost crucifix, scouring the house from top to bottom. Alas, it could not be found.

Bernice finally resigned herself to the fact that it must be gone forever.

■ ■ ■ ■

As Kristine walked past her old childhood home that early autumn morning, the memories flooded in. She missed her deceased mother even more than usual.

It was trash day, so Kristine wasn't surprised to see loaded containers at the curb in front of her childhood home.

Instead, she thought, *Imagine that, my mother's former house is again being gutted by new owners.*

Just then her foot kicked something. A little piece of trash from the pile went skittering along the street.

What is that? wondered Kristine, looking around.

Then the object came into view. It was propped against the curb, illuminated by a beam of light from the morning sun. She could hardly believe her eyes.

"No! It can't be!" she exclaimed with disbelief and joy.

It was impossible, yet there it was! Her dear mother's lost wooden crucifix!

Not only that, but as Kristine drew closer, she discovered that the display base the cross fit into . . . was right there beside it!

Where had it been hiding all those years?

No one will ever know.

But what Kristine *is* sure of is this: her path that morning was divinely aligned to connect with that lost crucifix, and that meant that God, probably in concert with her mother in heaven, orchestrated the whole thing!

Today, that little crucifix sits on Kristine's bedside table, reminding *her* of God's love and presence . . . and the need to pray.

Kristine still misses her mother terribly and wishes she could just pick up a phone and call her.

But now, when she passes her childhood home, she always recalls how God winked at her at that very special spot.

Think of it. That spot is a tiny dot on a globe made up of trillions of dots . . . and she never fails to whisper "Thank you, God" for the peace and joy He has given her because of that incredible Godwink . . . the reappearance of her mother's long-lost crucifix.

Reflections

Losing a mother is one of the deepest sorrows a heart can feel and when our moms are no longer here, we long for a sign . . . a heavenly connection.

What a comfort it was for Kristine to be

divinely led to something that was of such tangible value to her dear mother . . . the very crucifix that her mom had lifted to her heart while praying for each of her children. And only God knows how many times that tiny cross was stained with her mother's tears of worry.

It was also special that Kristine was reconnected to a treasure — so special to her mother — right in front of her childhood home.

It was a clear reminder for each of us that one day we will again hug and kiss our mothers . . . in their new homes in heaven.

God has prepared a final neighborhood for those who love Him — maybe it'll even be reminiscent of row houses, but where heavenly streets are lined with gold.

One of the greatest moments of pleasure will be your reunion with your mom . . . once again inhaling a bouquet that was unique to her . . . feeling the tenderness of her hand upon your cheek . . . and seeing the familiar joy in her eyes . . . the look you saw every time she welcomed you back home.

For we know that if the earthly tent we
live in is destroyed,

we have a building from God, an eternal
house in heaven,
not built by human hands.
— 2 CORINTHIANS 5:1 (NIV)

7B
Caroline — Mom's Yellow Car Peeve

Yellow is the brightest and happiest of colors — but Marie White hated it!

She didn't always hate it. Most of her life she was ambivalent about it. She simply liked other colors more . . . like a nice red or blue.

Yet, when the ninety-two-year-old became a resident of an assisted living facility in North Olmsted, Ohio, and developed dementia, with it came a strong aversion to — yellow.

And the greatest offender to her peace of mind was a yellow car!

When Marie and her daughter Caroline, who kept her on the go as much as they were both able, were on the road somewhere and deep in conversation, a yellow car crossing their path would trigger an almost Hulk-like response in gentle Marie. Not toward just anyone: she just needed to get it off her chest to Caroline how much she didn't like yellow!

Once the "offensive" vehicle was sighted, Marie would announce "Yellow car!" Then she was off to the races and on her soapbox. Caroline, compassionate and understanding, always listened patiently.

After Marie had vented thoroughly about the color, she would always recall a story involving her father and a car he had painted a yellowish-green decades ago when she was just a kid. Her father didn't like it and ended up painting it an entirely different color.

Because Marie recalled so little from her past, Caroline would patiently let her tell the story of her father and the long-ago summer of his yellow-green car . . . again and again and again.

After her mother passed away from complications of her dementia, Caroline missed her terribly. Even as her mom's illness progressed, Caroline and Marie had shared lots of laughs and good times together.

As the first anniversary of her mother's death approached in late August, Caroline was feeling her loss acutely . . . and longing for a sign from God that her mother was okay.

■ ■ ■ ■

One day Caroline was in a little fender-bender. No one was hurt, but she needed to take her car into the body shop for repair. Her auto insurance would cover a car rental for the time her car was being fixed.

So, on a bright and sunny morning before work, Caroline dropped her car off at the body shop on busy Lorain Boulevard and walked the short distance to a car rental business, where she had reserved a vehicle.

The "front" of the car rental place faced away from the boulevard so the brick back of the store is what she saw as she approached. She walked down the driveway along the side of the building and entered from the back.

At the counter, the car rental associate found her reservation. He noticed it was being covered by an insurance provider, so he took a chance at upselling.

"Are you sure you don't want to upgrade to a larger vehicle?"

"No, thank you. I'll only have it a few days while my car is being fixed."

Only a few days. But within those few days would be the one-year mark of her mother's graduation to heaven. She wouldn't need a fancy upgrade to go "joyriding" anywhere.

"Okay, that's fine. I've got your car in the lot across the street. You just wait outside here. And I'll pull it around."

She thanked him and did as he asked. Because she was standing at the back of the building, she couldn't see what car she was getting.

A few minutes later, she glanced down at her watch and then up again when she heard a car coming down the driveway along the side of the building. *That must be mine,* she thought.

He zipped around the corner of the building and pulled to a quick stop before her.

Her jaw dropped.

She laughed out loud. No way.

It was a YELLOW CAR!

Here was her bright and happy sign from God.

And just to punctuate her Godwink, when Caroline got into her cute, bright, *yellow car* and turned on the radio, her mom's only favorite song was playing — Anne Murray's "You Needed Me"!

A song from the seventies — not one you hear very often.

From that day forward, Caroline found

herself noticing yellow cars in traffic, just like her mom had. But for Caroline, every yellow car she spotted gave her a moment of peace and joy.

It was like getting a sunny little hello from above!

Reflections

God speaks to us in a personal language intended only for us to understand. For Caroline, it was yellow cars. For someone else, it might be a red bird's song or a blue butterfly's wings.

You just need to keep your heart and mind open to see the signs God gives you along your way . . . to strengthen and to guide you and, sometimes, just to say hello!

> Whether you turn to the right or to the left, your ears will hear a voice behind you, saying,
> "This is the way; walk in it."
> — Isaiah 30:21 (NIV)

7C
Yvonne and Vivian — Mother and Daughter — A Joyful Place

Vivian Shudde's upbeat voice lifted above the chatter and grabbed the attention of parents and friends gathered in the auditorium to enjoy one of the annual Open House Weekend's main attractions: a Christmas show starring thirty or forty of the "Citizens" residing at the Brookwood Community for Adults with Special Needs.

Attendees would soon be entertained by the highly lauded Brookwood Bell Choir, with each Citizen wearing a Santa hat, holding their bells at the ready, intently focused on their conductor.

Next would be an original play, always uplifting and delightful, highlighting the nurtured skills of every Citizen performer — often above and beyond their expectations — with a spirited sense of accomplishment.

Vivian, a humorous one-of-a-kind leader, had been CEO since her mother, Yvonne

Streit, Brookwood's founder, retired a decade or so earlier.

Her mother was a legendary force in the Houston area. Initially it was for founding a school for K–12 students with special challenges, which in part was to address the needs of her own daughter, Vicki, who at age one was severely brain damaged from encephalitis. Then, when Vicki reached her twenties, Yvonne met the stark reality facing every parent of a child with special needs: that few options exist to provide a fulfilling life for *adults* who are neurodiverse.

As a result, Yvonne Streit once again focused her true-grit leadership on establishing a solution — this time, Brookwood Community for Adults with Special Needs. As Vivian would later say with a smile, "You better listen to Mother . . . or you'll have footprints up your back."

It may seem unusual that two women — mother and daughter — would both be larger-than-life, projecting distinct and colorful personalities.

No one can doubt that they each played a major role in the evolution of Brookwood Community, located on 485 pastoral acres forty minutes west of Houston near Katy,

Texas. Today Brookwood is considered by many to be one of the premier organizations in the nation — perhaps the world — serving adults with special needs.

One of their missions is to share what they've learned with others. As of this writing, through Brookwood's Center for Learning, over three hundred organizations have visited the peaceful and picturesque campus, from every continent in the world except Antarctica, to learn the "Brookwood Way."

Vivian, as the sister of Vicki, remembers how that way began.

As a child, she recalls her mother having a sign-up sheet to enlist helpers with big hearts to put Vicki through a series of exercises to stimulate movement. She and other family members had one or two of those daily shifts.

"One of Mother's goals," Vivian explained, "was to teach Vicki how to feed herself. That meant she needed to learn to grasp something, lift it, and release it."

Parents with similar needs began showing up at Yvonne's home hoping she could be the answer to their prayers . . . to improve their children's lives. Pretty soon she was working with children in her backyard, who were learning to move on trampolines, climb ladders, crawl through canvas tubes — activities disguised as fun but teaching them to do things they never thought they could do.

That was what led to the founding of the Briarwood School, which continues to thrive today.

By the time Brookwood Community for Adults with Special Needs was founded, Vicki Streit was twenty-two and one of its earliest Citizens.

Says Vivian, "My sister's unique ability to 'grasp, lift and release' allowed Mother to put Vicki to work in the horticulture department. She could grasp a potted plant, lift it, and release it into its proper place on a tray."

Yvonne says, "Brookwood Citizens today propagate about 300,000 plants a year."[1] Therefore, one can only imagine how many of those plants may have been handled by Vicki during her four decades on the job!

Every year Brookwood grows an annual crop of approximately fifty thousand Christmas poinsettias, contributing to the reve-

1 Yvonne Streit, *Everyone's Got a Seed to Sow* (Bright Sky Press, 2016), 75.

nues generated by products made or grown by the Citizens. That enables Yvonne to maintain her original pledge not to take any government money. Instead they depend on revenue generated by Brookwood Community itself, as well as donations. Says Yvonne, "We are grateful and honor the kind people who help us address the needs of one of the most rapidly growing segments of society: special-needs adults."

Back to the Brookwood Christmas Show. As Vivian continued her enthusiastic greeting to those gathered for the Christmas show, one girl who was disabled, seated with her family, began to loudly cry out. Her parents tried to quiet her.

Vivian said, "She's fine. We're in their world now."

Once again, Vivian Shudde was demonstrating an acute ability to resonate with — and to defend — those whose minds and bodies are not the same as most, thereby underscoring the mission of Brookwood: "To Change the Worldview About Adults with Disabilities."

One tenet of the Brookwood culture is to treat every person with respect.

"We teach our Citizens that everyone is

famous for something," says Greg Glauser, the writer and director of every Christmas show for decades. "Our job is to help them find it and encourage it."

We learn that the Brookwood staff avoids using the word *normal.* With quick wit, Vivian would remind us, "Normal is just a setting on the dryer."

While Vivian's point of view evolved by growing up in a household with a severely disabled sister — as well as majoring in special education at college — she, like her mother, also learned the hard way. She gave birth to a son with special needs, Wilson.

Today Wilson, forty-one, is one of the most engaging residents on the Brookwood campus. Every one of the 114 full-time residents and 147 day students recognize the cheerful and distinctive voice of Wilson approaching . . . and he's never at a loss for conversation.

Vivian began wrapping up her Open House Weekend introduction.

"As you tour the Brookwood campus today you might see some people who are physically handicapped. You might see some who are mentally handicapped. But I challenge you to find anyone who is spiritually handicapped."

Looking seriously at the audience, she continued: "We believe God has called us to serve his *most* beloved children. As Proverbs tells us, 'Speak for those who have no voice.' "

To honor those with "no voice," Vivian is never at a loss. An endearing anecdote always seems to spring to her lips.

For instance, when one of Brookwood's Special Olympics basketball players shot a basket for the other team, the coach told him what he did.

He responded, "I know . . . they needed the points."

POSTSCRIPT

A beautiful twenty-minute documentary captured the experience of life on the Brookwood Community campus. The story is told through the distinct personalities of Yvonne and Vivian, along with many dedicated staff members, and most importantly by the joy-filled faces and voices of the Citizens.

"The Joy of Brookwood"[2] is an uplifting tribute to what a mother and daughter —

2 "A Joyful Place — The Brookwood Story,"

each with a special-needs child of their own — can do to help others in the same situation.

The inspiring journey is also described in the book *Everybody's Got a Seed to Sow,* by Yvonne Streit with Jana Mullins.

Personally, Louise and I know Brookwood very well. Our son Grant lives there.

REFLECTIONS

God's love for us is never measured by cognitive scores. He doesn't grade us on worldly achievements. God looks upon the heart.

In God's eyes, children with special needs are special. They have big hearts!

Ask any parent of a child with disabilities: most will admit it's challenging at times. Yet nearly every one of them will cheerfully tell you how enriched their lives have become . . . how their special-needs child has taught them to be more accepting, understanding, and compassionate toward others.

Yvonne and Vivian trusted God to write their story with them, even though it wasn't the one they would have chosen. Every

---

trailer, YouTube, https://www.youtube.com/watch?v=XSPpQgnA2gc

obstacle they encountered was overcome by their uncompromising faith and persistence.

When visitors enter the Brookwood Community they see the childlike pureness and unconditional love that each Citizen brings to every person they meet.

> Now to the one who can do infinitely more than all we can ask or imagine according to the power that is working among us.
>
> — EPHESIANS 3:20 (ISV)

Yvonne and Vivian's greatest aim is to teach Citizens that they each have a purpose — a job for God.

Oftentimes, however, it's been the Citizens who are the teachers about the love of Christ. They have been the encouragers showing Yvonne and Vivian — and all the Brookwood teachers — that they can indeed make a difference in how the world views adults with disabilities.

7D
Kathryn and Ruth — We'll Always Be Close

The sun was setting in Redondo Beach, California, as dolphins appeared, playing in the surf. Kathryn Dow, an aspiring screenwriter in her early thirties, watched them until the sun slipped past the horizon, and the sky was awash in color.

She could no longer put off the call she'd been dreading since she left the doctor's office that morning. It would be well after dinnertime in Ohio, and she knew she'd catch her mother at home.

Although they were close — in fact, it was because they were close, even though thousands of miles separated them — Kathryn hadn't told her mother about the almond-shaped lump she'd found on her neck. Her mother was still grieving the sudden loss of her husband, Charles — Kathryn's father — three years earlier. Kathryn didn't want to give her something else to worry about.

Her first thought was that she would tell

her after she determined everything was okay.

But then, after a rushed series of tests and a meeting with a specialist that day, a needle biopsy was ordered. It was Thursday. The biopsy was scheduled for Monday.

Kathryn now felt it was only fair to prepare her mom, in case the results weren't good.

At home in Cleveland, her mother, Ruth Dow, a woman in her late seventies, answered on the second ring. Kathryn would later joke that after she told her mom her news, "She just left the receiver hanging and headed for the airport and the next flight to Los Angeles!"

In fact, Ruth arrived on Saturday. She wanted to be with her daughter for the biopsy.

Ruth stayed for two months, through the surgery to remove the cancerous tumor and subsequent treatment. When Kathryn wasn't allowed to drive, she was so proud of the way her nearly eighty-year-old mother managed to drive across town in the infamous and unforgiving LA traffic.

Even though it wasn't an easy time, the two

made the best of it, finding moments of fun where they could — going out to eat, visiting Huntington Gardens to restage a photo her mother had taken on a trip to Pasadena when she was young, and then, of course, watching tons of rom-coms, their favorite kind of movie.

Ruth was surprised to learn Kathryn had never seen *You've Got Mail,* which had been released six months earlier. Somehow, in the nonstop whirlwind of working as a script coordinator in television production, that movie had slipped through the cracks.

Ruth wouldn't rest until they picked up a copy at the video store and watched it together. She knew with absolute certainty it would be Kathryn's "cup of tea," and of course she was right. Kathryn loved it. Even more, she loved the fact her mother knew how much she would.

Best of all, getting caught up in the troubles of Kathleen Kelly, the film's heroine, made the two forget their own for a little while.

After her mother returned home, Kathryn tried to return to business as usual. Before her cancer diagnosis, she had just signed with a wonderful, up-and-coming literary agent, who was busy lining up exciting meetings for her.

But now, with her health a concern, she knew she couldn't return to the exciting but exhausting daily grind of television production. And with her father gone, her mother would benefit greatly from Kathryn's return to Ohio. Writing for television and movies was one dream, but she wondered if it was now time to pursue some others. She looked for a sign to point her in the right direction.

Friends and family in Ohio urged her to return home.

On one such call with her mother, Kathryn said, "I would go back to Ohio, but I have another year on my apartment lease."

A knock on the door interrupted her call. It was the man who owned the condo she rented. He explained he was having a tough time and needed to move back into his condo. But he knew they had a lease, and he would honor it. He only wanted to let her know that, if she wanted to get out of the lease now for any reason, it would be fine with him.

Wow. Kathryn was stunned. There was her sign. Did she need it in writing? God was winking. And giving her the chance to go home.

After ten incredible years in Los Angeles,

Kathryn said goodbye to the good friends she had made and the life she knew and loved. Her agent was sorry she was leaving and promised she would always read anything Kathryn wrote (a promise she has kept to this day).

After several treatments in Ohio, Kathryn's cancer was in remission. She found a job she loved as a full-time greeting card writer and editor, and, in her "spare" time, she wrote rom-com movie scripts with her friend John, who also worked at the greeting card company.

Kathryn and her mother shared lots of laughs and great times together, going to movies, and indulging in one of their favorite pastimes — going out to eat. On more than one occasion, strangers paid for their bill.

Most did so anonymously, but one man approached them to explain. Ruth reminded him of his own mother, whom he missed dearly. He said he felt compelled to do this act of kindness "for my mom, because she raised me right."

A few years after Kathryn returned home, Ruth's memory began to fail. But her sense of humor never did. When Kathryn explained that a CT scanner was going to take a picture of her brain, she replied, "I hope they can find it!"

Ruth was diagnosed with vascular dementia. Kathryn was grateful she could be there for her mother, who moved into an assisted living apartment just around the corner from her.

As the years and disease progressed, Ruth lived in the moment and loved to share a laugh. She might not remember some things, but she always knew when they were going out to dinner or their weekly Sunday brunch.

It was after such a brunch at one of their favorite places that they would pull out of the parking lot and wait at a red light, which faced an old 1920s movie theater converted into a pub.

Kathryn would explain that she and her writing partner met there regularly to write their rom-com script about a greeting card writer. It seemed like a good idea to write a movie in a place that had once been a movie theater. Kathryn mentioned this a few times and then found that, despite the dementia, her mom remembered it the next week, and the week after that.

As they waited for the light to turn green, it was her mom who would bring it up. "Isn't that where you write your script?"

She'd want to hear the latest update.

In the spring of the following year, Ruth's health was failing rapidly. During moments when she was at her sickest, she would sometimes confuse Kathryn for her own mother, and of course Kathryn didn't correct her. In a way, she was right — the loving bond was the same.

The weather on Mother's Day was sunny and gorgeous, as they sat in a beautiful garden in bloom on the nursing home's grounds. Kathryn knew it would be the last Mother's Day they shared, and because their time together was growing so short, Kathryn felt compelled to say, "No matter where we are, we'll always be close." Kathryn didn't expect Ruth's response.

"That's exactly what your father keeps telling me."

Kathryn's father, who had been gone now for over a decade.

"No matter where we are, we'll always be close."

It was something Kathryn had said to her mother to give her some comfort. Instead it proved to be a source of great comfort to Kathryn in the years following Ruth's death.

■ ■ ■ ■

Two years later, in the spring, Kathryn was under a great deal of stress, both bad and good. Bad — there were reasons to believe her cancer may have returned. Good — the rom-com script she and her writing partner worked on years before in the old-movie-theater-turned-pub was getting a "blinking green light" from a network.

There was an executive at the network asking for a new outline for the script. If the changes were approved, the blinking light would turn solid green. It would be good to go for production, and a dream of a lifetime would come true for Kathryn.

But hey, no pressure.

On the night before the medical procedure that would determine whether the cancer was back, Kathryn was also on a deadline to finish her pass at the new script outline. To make matters worse, her old laptop computer would freeze and crash several times an hour, requiring a lengthy reboot process.

As she was typing away, lost in the story, it happened again. Frozen. She was tempted to throw the laptop out the window, but she realized that wouldn't really help her situation.

This time she decided she wouldn't watch it slowly reboot as her frustration steadily grew. Instead she would use this time to try to calm down and "reboot" herself.

She breathed deeply and averted her gaze from the screen, looking at the floor instead. And she prayed. For good health. For inspired writing that would turn a blinking light to solid green. She prayed for hope and comfort and peace in her heart. She spent so much time in this posture that when she looked up, the computer had finished rebooting.

And she was startled to see she was looking directly into the smiling face of her mother, Ruth, on the screen!

She recognized the photo as one of her favorites — she and her mother sharing a dessert at the Cheesecake Factory. The photo was not open when the computer had frozen. It was not a screensaver. It was just one of many photos in her photo gallery. But no other photo appeared on the screen. And though Kathryn was in the photo as well, an operating systems graphic covered that part, so only Ruth was visible to her.

"No matter where we are, we'll always be close."

■ ■ ■ ■

During the years when Ruth's health declined, she was a great patient — upbeat and kind. But if a doctor or nurse pushed her too hard, she would say in a strong and stern voice, "You're hurting me."

In other words, knock it the heck off.

As Kathryn was undergoing the medical procedure the next day, there was a moment just before the pain even registered with her when she "heard" her mother's voice loudly say, "You're hurting me."

The tech responded, "Oh, I'm sorry!" Yet not a word or whimper had been uttered. She repositioned Kathryn in such a way that the pain disappeared. Had she heard her mom's voice reprimanding her too?!

The test results were ready immediately and gave welcome news — no cancer!

With great relief, Kathryn realized she hadn't eaten all day and headed to a nearby diner. She was reviewing the new script outline (which would later be approved and given a green light — yay!) when she noticed that a mother and her adult daughter were seated in the booth just ahead of her.

They were chatting excitedly and laughing

with each other. While Kathryn couldn't make out everything they said, it was clear they had just purchased a condominium together and were reviewing all the things they still needed to do. Shopping lists and fun, galore.

On Kathryn's way out of the diner, she paid her bill — and theirs — smiling as she thought, *For my mom, because she raised me right.*

Postscript

When their holiday rom-com movie premiered on TV in December of that year, Kathryn and her writing partner, John, hosted a watch party with family and friends at the old converted theater where they had worked on the script.

The pub put the name of their movie on the old marquee above the entrance.

It was the same one Ruth and Kathryn would look at as they waited for the traffic light to change to green. And her mother would say, "Isn't that where you write your script?"

Life's a circle.

REFLECTIONS

Sometimes you need to take a step back to step forward.

In some ways, it felt like Kathryn was quitting her dream when she left Los Angeles, but she was really saying yes to taking better care of herself and those she loved, especially her mother.

God gave her the chance to heal and recover and discover new paths and new people. And God didn't give up on the Hollywood dream He put in her heart. He just took her on the scenic route to get there.

So, it's okay if your dreams evolve and change or take some time to grow — enjoy the view! And know God is with you every step of the way.

Life may not always be easy, but remember you're not alone . . . even though it may sometimes feel like you are.

With God's grace, your journey is blessed with people He puts in your path — for you to love and be loved by along the way. They make the road a little easier, more worthwhile, and much more fun to navigate.

Remember that God is with you in the good times and the bad times, for all time.

No matter where you are, He will always

be close.

> I have commanded you to be determined and confident!
> Do not be afraid or discouraged, for I, the LORD your God,
> am with you wherever you go.
> — JOSHUA 1:9 (GNT)

8
Moms and Angel Encounters

8A
Roma —
Hugged by an Angel

Sometimes God uses each of us as Godwink Links — unwitting messengers of a Godwink to someone else.

For what purpose? Maybe just to be a light of reassurance, to comfort them, or let them know they are not alone.

The young woman approached Roma with a look of shyness, yet also determination. It was common for people to recognize Roma Downey. After all, her television series took her into twenty million homes every week.

"I want you to know that you helped save my life," said the young woman, her voice shaking slightly.

"How was that?" responded Roma, in her kindly Irish brogue.

The woman raised her wrists for Roma to see — her pale skin reddened around the scars.

"I . . . was taking my own life," she said,

hesitantly. "I felt abandoned . . . by my family and by God. I was bleeding, my back against the bathroom wall, sliding down, collapsing on the floor, waiting to die."

She paused . . . swallowing a flood of tears . . .

"I shouted, 'Even now there is no word from you, God, because you are not there!' "

She sucked in a breath as her eyes widened, looking directly at Roma.

"Then I heard you speak. You said: 'You are not alone. You have never been alone. Don't you know that God loves you?' "

Trying to grasp the situation — what the young woman was talking about — Roma looked at her sympathetically; fearing anything she said — that was flashing through her mind — could sound harsh.

You heard me? she asked in her thoughts. *Where? When? I don't understand.*

It was not unusual for Roma, who played the lead angel on the TV series *Touched by an Angel,* to encounter fans who felt as though they knew her like a neighbor or close friend, or, in some cases, thinking that she was a "real" angel.

But this was different . . . this young woman said *she heard* her?

A stark silence hung in the air as Roma

looked deeply into the girl's eyes and again watched her swallow away tears.

It was a surreal millisecond.

Then God gave Roma clarity . . . an understanding of what must have occurred.

As impossible as it would seem, God must have divinely aligned Roma's voice on a *Touched by an Angel* program to be heard by this poor woman, at the very moment she was lost in despair and needed someone to love her . . . and to tell her so.

Roma calculated that from a television set in another room . . . the very instant the young woman was about to permanently harm herself . . . crying out to God one last time . . . she must have heard the "angel revelation segment" written into every show. That was the tender scene in every script when the actor playing an angel revealed themselves to someone in trouble.

"It was you," continued the young woman, her voice cracking, "until that moment I didn't even know the TV was on. In answer to my cry for God to show Himself to me, I heard your voice!" The woman's final words merged into a sobbing cry.

Arrested in astonishment, Roma's mind wondered what unbelievable odds must have been required for such a Godwink to unfold — considering the thousands and thousands of hours of programming on television — and for Roma's recorded voice to come out of a TV — located in a place where this desperate soul could hear a handful of words, spoken in earnest, to the very person God wanted to save.

And now, another Godwink of divine alignment. Here was that very young woman encountering Roma in person!

The woman's voice, continuing — stronger now — was bringing Roma back to the present.

"I wrapped my wrists in a towel and called for an ambulance," she said with a sigh, "and that's how you saved my life."

Roma looked at her with compassion and managed a whispered response.

"And *that* is evidence that angels are the messengers of an ever-present God."

Both choking back tears, Roma reached out to the young woman and held her.

A sense of peace came over the two of them as an awareness crept into their minds that God's Love Light was shining upon them, ever so tenderly, as invisible threads were connecting them — not by accident but by divine alignment — on His "GPS": God's Positioning System.

"Imagine that," said Roma smiling, while holding the young woman by the shoulders.

"My voice, as Monica the angel, coming through a television set in another room, at perhaps the most crucial moment of your life, to bring you hope and assurance of God's love, just when you needed it. That's just like Him, isn't it?"

They hugged again.

REFLECTIONS

God calls us to be His hands, feet, and heart here on earth. He also often calls us to be His voice.

Roma's lilting Irish brogue spoke words of comfort and reassurance right from the throne room in heaven . . . to the TV in the room adjacent to this young woman . . . to deliver a lifesaving message. He longed for her to know, in her most desperate moment, that she was not abandoned . . . but in fact loved very much.

Through Roma, on a TV, He spoke life into her.

Is there someone in your life whom God has used to be a vessel, thereby giving *you* a message of hope and comfort? A *yes* answer would not be unusual.

We will never be perfect enough to represent God, but here's the good news: we don't have to be. God wants *willing vessels.*

He doesn't call the equipped; He equips the called.

When we make it a habit to listen for His voice, we can sense his presence. He will reveal himself. Then, just maybe, He will use you to be someone's Godwink Link — the unwitting deliverer of a Godwink to someone else, just as he used Roma.

> Come near to God and he will come near to you.
>
> — James 4:8 (NIV)

8B
Carrie — Angels at the Door

It's been twenty years now. But Carrie Hinely remembers it like it was yesterday — that sunny, seemingly ordinary Saturday afternoon that soon became anything but.

A wife, and mother of three boys, Carrie, along with her husband, Chris, ran a thriving business in Columbia, South Carolina: the Peanut Man gift shop and candy store.

To say Carrie Hinely was a busy woman would be an understatement.

But despite her hectic schedule, Carrie juggled her myriad responsibilities with unwavering grace and good humor. So, when her eight-year-old son, Mitchell, a skateboard aficionado, asked for a ride to the park, Carrie told him to grab his board and helmet. She would drop him off to skate for an hour while she ran some errands and stopped at work.

A fairly new addition to town, the skateboard park was close to everything, clean and well supervised — a place where parents could feel safe about dropping their kids off for some fun.

Carrie checked Mitchell in, signed the release, and made her son give her a pinky promise to keep his helmet on while grinding the rails.

Then off she went.

She was standing in her store when the phone rang. It was the skateboard park. Mitchell had fallen on the back of his head and needed to go to the emergency room.

Though he had been wearing his helmet, the little boy had been knocked out cold when he fell. The park workers urged Carrie to come get him and have him checked out, even though Mitchell said he felt fine. So Carrie called Chris and they rushed Mitchell to the ER.

After what seemed to be a lifetime, the examining doctor came out to talk with the worried parents. But what he had to say brought them no comfort.

Though Mitchell seemed fine from the fall, the MRI revealed a cyst on the back of the boy's brain. There was no way of knowing how long it had been there, just that it was in evidence now, and quite possibly growing. They would need to keep a close eye on it.

Mitchell was prescribed medication and scheduled for an MRI every three months.

That was the easy part.

Soon he began experiencing excruciating migraines and started losing his vision. Before long he was unable to go to school, play with his friends, or even watch TV.

Each MRI revealed an expansion of the tumor's growth.

The doctors started discussing surgery. But Carrie and Chris felt uneasy about someone cutting into their son's brain.

"Isn't there anything else we can try?" she asked.

The doctors said they could immediately start Mitchell on a different protocol of medicine.

Meanwhile, Carrie and Chris continued praying for their son — alone, together, and with their respective support groups at church.

Then, one Sunday afternoon, there was a knock on their door.

Chris opened it to find Peter and Toni — a husband and wife from their church — asking if they could come in and pray for Mitchell.

Aging hippies, Peter was tall and lanky and carried a velvet satchel while Toni had long blond hair, flowing over her shoulders, and kind green eyes. Both sported numerous tattoos and their motorcycle was behind them in the driveway.

Chris recognized Peter from his support group, as Carrie recognized Toni from hers. They were new in town and had been coming to their church for two or three months.

"May we come in and pray for your son?" asked Peter.

"We won't stay long," Toni assured them.

Carrie and Chris looked at each other and nodded in agreement. They believed in prayer, and although they didn't know Peter and Toni well, they knew them well enough to let them in.

So Mitchell was brought to the living room, and Peter and Toni got ready.

It was unlike anything Carrie or Chris had ever experienced.

Peter retrieved incense from his satchel and lit it, and while swinging a brass ball on a chain over Mitchell's head, he and Toni began to pray — fervently — first in English, then in tongues, something Carrie and Chris had read about but never witnessed.

After fifteen minutes, Peter asked if there were any other children at home. So Mitchell's brothers Jared and Matt were brought in. Peter and Toni prayed over those children, then over the entire family.

When they were finished, Peter put everything back into his velvet bag, winked at Carrie and Chris, and told them, "Everything is fine."

Sensing their skepticism, Toni smiled warmly.

"Not to worry . . . you'll see soon . . . he's healed," she said matter-of-factly.

They walked out the door, climbed onto their Harley, and rode away.

Carrie and Chris stayed awake, talking in bed, until at least two in the morning.

"What in the world just happened in our home?" they pondered.

The next morning, they got up and went to their support groups; neither Peter nor Toni was there. But it wasn't unusual for someone to miss a meeting. That happened all the time.

Peter and Toni missed the next week's meeting too.

Now, a week or two after the hippie couple's visit, it was time for Mitchell's MRI. It had been a year and a half since the tumor was discovered and these MRIs every three months were becoming routine.

During this visit, the doctor said, "Really, the only thing that's going to heal your son . . . the only person who can do that . . .

is God."

"It's funny you should say that," said Carrie. "Some people came by the house to pray for him. They told us they didn't think surgery would be necessary."

"We really feel that Mitchell is going to get over this with prayer and God," Chris agreed.

Then . . . over the next three months that's exactly what happened! It was astonishing — Mitchell improved noticeably!

He went outside, running and playing with his friends — things he hadn't been able to do in over a year.

After that his vision started getting better . . . enough that he could watch television again and go back to school.

As a result, Carrie and Chris grew more and more hopeful.

Then, two days after Mitchell's next MRI, they got a phone call: "The doctor needs to see you," the nurse said solemnly.

Carrie and Chris panicked.

They waited anxiously in the doctor's office; when he came in, his eyes were tearing up.

Chris reached for Carrie's hand as they braced for bad news.

"I don't know what's happened," said the

astounded physician. "But there's no sign of a tumor in Mitchell's brain. Zero. It's completely gone."

Carrie and Chris began crying. Then laughing. Then crying and laughing together, unsure of what was happening or how they were feeling.

"I'd like to do another MRI today," said the doctor. "Just to be sure."

But . . . when the MRI report came in, no abnormalities were found!

"I'm going to wean him off his medications," said the doctor, astonished. "By the grace of God, Mitchell's tumor is gone!"

Carrie and Chris couldn't stop praising and thanking God.

They still can't; twenty years later, Mitchell is tumor-free!

No one's ever seen Peter or Toni again. They never returned to the Hinelys' church or their prayer groups.

"They were angels," Carrie declares with complete conviction. "They didn't look spiritual, at least not in the way most people expect. But they were angels."

Now a grown man, Mitchell remains healthy and tumor-free. He and his family have shared his story countless times with people who are facing seemingly hopeless situations; it always increases their faith.

If Mitchell hadn't hit his head at the skate park, the tumor would have continued to grow.

But it *was* found.

And Mitchell was healed.

Carrie and her family always smile when remembering another blessing that extraordinary day they were angelically visited by Toni and Peter.

That wink from Peter — as he said "Everything is fine" just before Toni added "You'll see soon that he's healed" — was a Godwink from above.

REFLECTIONS

When the doctor told Carrie and Chris that their little boy's fall had revealed a growth in his brain, they were shocked.

Their faith was repeatedly tested as they navigated a frightening period of uncertainty over the following months. A terrible burden for any family.

Yet with hindsight, they could clearly see that if Mitchell had not fallen, striking the back of his head, the doctors might not have found the tumor in time.

With God, there is nothing by chance. Even with those things that are hidden or unplanned.

Very often God's handiwork becomes evident later, just as He told us in the ancient scriptures:

> In all things, God works for the good of those who love him,
> who have been called according to His purpose.
>
> — ROMANS 8:28 (NIV)

That verse reassures us that God uses even the worst of times for His goodness . . . and "the good of those who love him."

The reaffirmation is also comforting: that as we pour out our hearts in prayer — as Carrie and Chris did — God hears us.

Sometimes He sends invisible angels to help, and once in a great while people show up who bear the resemblance of heavenly creatures among us . . . to bring Godwinks and miracles.

> God will command his angels to protect you wherever you go.
>
> — PSALM 91:11 (CEV)

8C
Brittany II — Nanny's Thanksgiving Angel

Studying to be an astrophysicist is hard.

Studying to be an astrophysicist in your thirties with a family and a full-time job is light-years harder.

Brittany Alford knew this because it was exactly what she was doing, and she was crushing it. She took a moment to look up from her quantum mathematics textbook.

For Brittany, her study of science only strengthened her faith in God. How could you look at the images of the universe coming back from the James Webb Space Telescope and not see God?

The cherub bookends on the shelf caught her eye.

Each ivory-colored bookend was an angel child standing in an open palm of God — a boy on one side and a girl on the other. She cherished them because they had belonged to Nanny Linda, the grandmother she adored and missed dearly.

Nanny Linda lived a life of unwavering faith. She loved angels and anything about them, from songs and books to movies and mugs. In fact, Nanny was the easiest person in the family to shop for . . . on any occasion!

As a little girl, Brittany always wondered why Nanny loved angels so much. One day she asked her.

"Because I saw one. And she saved our lives," Nanny Linda replied matter-of-factly, and left it at that.

When Brittany and her cousin Ashley were about twelve years old and on summer break from middle school, they were thrilled to have a sleepover at Nanny Linda's. They loved spending time with her. And it didn't hurt that she made the absolute best biscuits in the world.

There was always a sense of peace and happiness at her home in Canton, Georgia, no doubt enhanced by the angelic décor.

As the girls helped Nanny make dinner, Brittany again wondered about the roots of her grandmother's infatuation with angels. So she asked.

Nanny Linda looked at Brittany and Ashley, sizing them up, wondering, *Are they old enough to understand what happened to me on a fateful Thanksgiving Day decades ago?*

After a moment, she decided they were. She stopped peeling the potatoes and told the girls to do the same. She wiped her hands on a kitchen towel — emblazoned with an angel, of course.

She asked the girls to get three glasses down from the cabinet while she got ice and a pitcher of fresh lemonade from the refrigerator. She poured them each a glass.

"Let's go into the living room, relax a minute, and I'll tell you."

"Yes, ma'am!"

The girls sat on the couch opposite their grandmother's chair. They had never seen her so serious before — they knew she was about to tell them something important. They sat on the edge of their seats. An excited chill ran through Brittany.

Then Nanny Linda began to speak about that memorable day some fifty years before as if it were yesterday . . .

She explained that the cabin where they lived at the time was just off the road in a remote part of Alabama. The surrounding area was flat, and you could see for miles, in all directions.

They didn't know anyone, and no neighbors were in sight. Just the long dirt road and fields on both sides.

Her father, Jack, had moved the family there from Georgia because he was offered work in town.

At the time, Nanny Linda was eight, the oldest of three children — she had a four-year-old brother, Stanley, and a baby sister, Brenda.

Life was very hard. Their dad was an abusive alcoholic, and when he drank too much, which was often, he would hit their mother, Anna Belle.

Young Linda did the best she could to help her mom by watching out for her younger siblings.

They had only been in their new home in Alabama for a few days when Dad went on another drinking binge.

He drunkenly threatened to take the car and desert them, leaving them stranded in the cabin, in an unfamiliar area with no means to take care of themselves — no food, no heat, no money, and not even a phone to call for help!

While he made things terribly difficult when he was around, his absence, at that vulnerable moment, would have been even harder to bear. Their mom honestly didn't know how they would survive without him. She begged him not to go.

But he did go. He walked out the door

and drove off. They never saw him again.

The next day was Thanksgiving.

The temperature dipped into the thirties. They were cold and hungry. It seemed they had very little to be thankful for, but . . . they had each other.

Stanley was hungry and started to cry.

Feeling totally helpless, Anna Belle rushed into the other room so the children wouldn't see her cry. But Linda could hear her through the door. She loved her mom so much and fervently wanted her to feel safe and loved.

That's when Linda had an idea. She knew exactly what to do. She would pray. She gathered the kids together, holding hands — Stanley on one side and Brenda on the other — and bowed her head.

"Please, God, our mommy needs your help. Please, please, God, bless our family — my mom, Stanley, Brenda, and me. It's Thanksgiving, and we're *sooo* hungry, God!"

Not even a minute later, there was a knock on the door.

Linda looked up. "Who could that be?" she asked with astonishment, like a little adult.

She opened the door to find a sweet and kind-looking lady standing there. She radiated a soothing and calm spirit, and Linda felt instantly comforted in her presence.

"Linda?" the lady asked in a gentle voice.

"Yes, ma'am."

"I have Thanksgiving dinner for you, honey."

Beside her were boxes of food and groceries.

"Oh, oh my," gasped Anna Belle, who had joined Linda at the door.

"Oh look, Mommy!" said Linda, jumping up and down, and suddenly realizing the two little kids were crowded in, squealing and jumping with her.

"Here, let me help you," said Anna Belle to the lady, picking up one box while Linda lifted the other, carrying them into the house.

"That's so wonderful of you," said Anna Belle, turning quickly back to the open door.

But there was no one there.

"Wait! We have to thank you," said Anna Belle as she rushed to the door, Linda right behind, echoing her mother's gratitude.

No one was on the porch. No one was in the yard, or in the drive. No car was driving away up the long dirt road.

The kind lady was gone.

Linda and her mom ran off the porch,

looking in all directions, for miles around them.

There was no sweet and kind woman anywhere. Anna Belle and the three children were all alone.

But they weren't really alone: God was watching over them and had blessed them with a Thanksgiving Angel especially for them!

As Linda looked up at her mom, with a wide smile of little-girl joy, she said, "Mommy, that nice lady came to the door right after we prayed."

Linda grasped her mother around the waist and allowed her little-girl tears to come pouring out.

There was so much food! With the kids pitching in to help, Anna Belle set the table and they had the most wonderful Thanksgiving dinner, with all the trimmings — turkey, gravy and mashed potatoes, beans, cranberry sauce, and, of course, pumpkin pie!

But before diving in, they were like a family in a Norman Rockwell painting — all bowing their heads in prayer, thanking God for His amazing grace.

Nanny Linda gazed at Brittany and Ashley,

whose jaws had dropped.

She smiled, quietly satisfied that she had finally shared this secret blessing, knowing it was now handed off to Brittany and Ashley to be preserved in the hearts of future family members.

"What happened next?" asked Nanny rhetorically.

Both girls excitedly nodded yes; they wanted to know.

"That food lasted until a relative arrived the following week to drive them back home to Georgia. Our Thanksgiving Angel had saved us and provided."

"Wow," said Brittany.

"Are you sure she wasn't a really nice neighbor or something?" inquired Ashley.

"No . . . we knew no one . . . and besides, a neighbor couldn't have vanished like that."

Nanny squeezed her lips together, smiling at the same time as if she were looking at a picture in her mind. "Nope. She was an angel, sent to answer my prayer. She knew where we lived and what we needed. She even knew my name."

Nanny Linda wiped a tear.

"I'm as certain that she was an angel as I am . . . that I have the best grandkids in the world."

Brittany and Ashley rushed to their grandmother and gave her the biggest hug.

REFLECTIONS

When life is hard, you're at the end of your rope, you fear for the safety of loved ones and yourself, and the cupboard is hopelessly bare — God is with you.

His angels protect you and provide for you. And just like those cherished cherub bookends in Brittany's living room, He holds you in the palm of His hand.

Even in a cabin, on a dusty road, in an unfamiliar place, with no one in sight.

Young Linda and her family were far from home. Alone and scared. They had no idea where they were, but God did.

When she called out to God for help — in her little-girl voice — He heard her. And came to the rescue of her family, subsequently delivering them safely home to Georgia, where they continued to build a loving family for generations to come, sharing God's love every step of the way.

It may sometimes be easier said than done, but even in hard times, fear not — ask for help! God and His angels are with you always!

from heaven . . .

— LUKE 22:43 (KJV)

8D
Mary Jo — Angels for Exhausted Mom

It was the happiest day of Mary Jo Chambers's life: the day she brought her baby daughter, Melanie, home from the hospital.

She marveled at what a fighter little Melanie was and often stood over her crib, just listening to her breathe, and thanking God for entrusting her to mother this sweet child.

Yet, despite her baby's natural disposition, she had had a rough start in life. Born with severely dislocated hips and club feet, her tiny body had undergone more than a dozen major surgeries by the time she was just seven months old.

Melanie's movements were always restricted, held in place by casts, braces, and harnesses, making it nearly impossible for her child to get any sleep.

That meant that *Mary Jo* got no sleep!

As weeks without sleep turned into months,

Mary Jo knew she needed a miracle. The exhaustion lay upon her like a heavy blanket, to the point where she sometimes found herself dozing off while standing up.

On a typical night, she got up repeatedly. Whenever Melanie let out a cry or a whimper, she would have to rock her for hours.

Her husband was little help. Tending to a child wasn't in his skill set. Besides, he had to be rested for his job. So that left her on her own.

Mary Jo knew she couldn't continue this way. Tears welled up within her. She fell to her knees and begged God for help.

"Oh God, I'm so blessed and grateful that you chose me to be the mother of this precious child. She's such a gift, and I will never, ever take it for granted how fortunate I am.

"But God . . ." She paused to allow her convulsing body to gulp with sobs. ". . . I'm just so tired."

Tears streamed down her cheeks. "Please, God, please send your angels to take care of my little baby so I can get one good night's sleep. I don't know how long I can go on."

When her child finally quieted for a few moments, Mary Jo wiped her tears, got up, and walked zombielike to the kitchen.

She opened the refrigerator and began her nightly ritual of preparing a bottle to have it ready during the night.

Mary Jo yawned, almost stumbling from exhaustion, and trudged to her bedroom, falling into the bed next to her husband, who was already sound asleep.

She would never remember her head hitting the pillow. Her sleep was like a total blackout. In fact, it was the most uninterrupted sleep her body had felt in the multiple weeks since the baby was born.

At 2 a.m. her baby expelled a tiny whimper. Mary Jo bolted up . . . looked at the clock . . . shocked that she had been asleep for six hours!

That never happens, she thought, tumbling quickly out of bed.

She went directly to check on Melanie and was astonished by what she saw. Melanie, with her pink blanket and stuffed bunny, was sleeping peacefully!

And next to her was the bottle . . . the one from the refrigerator . . . nearly gone!

What??

Mary Jo stood in the nursery staring at Melanie's sweet sleeping face, which held the hint of a smile, like she was having the best dream ever . . . and then she felt the Lord tell her that He'd answered her prayer. The angels were watching over Melanie . . . she should go back to sleep.

The feeling was one of overwhelming joy, but also disbelief.

When Mary Jo returned to the bedroom, her husband was stirring. So she asked him if he had gotten up and given Melanie her bottle.

He looked at her oddly and shook his head no.

Mary Jo told him what happened.

"Are you sure it wasn't you . . . half-asleep?"

She shook her head.

He was so freaked-out, he jumped out of bed and ran to turn on all the lights!

He said, "If it wasn't you who gave Melanie the bottle, and it wasn't me, then who was it?"

Mary Jo couldn't help smiling, quickly telling her husband she wasn't laughing at him . . . but she felt a huge surge of peacefulness and satisfaction. God was listening to her.

She had prayed for Him to send angels to watch over her baby, so she could catch up on sleep . . . and that's exactly what He did!

In fact, Melanie was *still* sleeping. So Mary Jo crawled right back under the covers and slept for another three hours.

Reflections

Mary Jo got a great rest that night, and so did Melanie. Those angels must have been humming nursery rhymes and rocking her to sleep all night long.

Moms know how to juggle life, but they often don't know how to manage sleep. Lack of rest drains the body and can be physically and emotionally harmful.

If you're sleep-deprived, surrender all your worries and anxieties to God. He is your ultimate source of comfort and strength.

Mary Jo prayed . . . and God answered . . . He sent angels to stand guard for little Melanie, giving her rest for her weary mind and body.

He will do the same for you!

> Come to me, all you who are weary and burdened, and I will give you rest.
>
> — Matthew 11:28 (NIV)

9
Grandmoms Are Great!

9A
SUSAN — *WHEEL OF FORTUNE* TWINS

Susan Assenzo entered Kitty's Restaurant in North Reading, Massachusetts, for her weekly lunch with one of her best friends, Jean.

Both were now grandparents in their sixties, though they had been friends since high school, when they worked together as cashiers at Star Market, a grocery store in their hometown of Stoneham.

Susan spotted Jean, already seated, and gave her a wave as she headed to their table.

Jean stood up and gave her friend a quick hug before they both settled in.

"Did you see *Wheel of Fortune* last night?"

"Yes! I can't believe that guy missed such an easy answer!"

Their faces registered their mutual dismay.

"I know! But it must be so hard to be up there, in front of an audience and under all those lights. I don't think I could do it."

Susan nodded as it flashed through her

mind how *Wheel* had become an integral part of her friendship with Jean — as well as her whole family.

Back when she and her husband, Dennis, were first dating, they joked that it was a crazy coincidence to discover that both of their moms and dads were wild about a nightly TV game show . . . *Wheel of Fortune.*

Who could have imagined that as she and Dennis grew older, they would fall right into line, taking on the dual family obsession — rarely missing their favorite TV show?

You could add to that obsession their boundless love for grandchildren.

As a grandparent herself now, Susan understood just how deeply that love went. She would move heaven and earth for her "grandbabies" and she and Dennis leapt at every opportunity to be with them.

Weeks later, Susan and Dennis were watching *Wheel of Fortune* one evening when their daughter Ashley called. Susan paused the show and put the call on speaker.

Ashley wondered if her parents could watch Leo, their two-year-old grandson, for an afternoon later that week.

Without even checking their calendars Susan and Dennis simultaneously answered, "Absolutely!"

■ ■ ■ ■

Three days later they were giddy at the chance to have their grandson all to themselves. It was a fun day. But Susan and Dennis had no idea how great a day it was going to be.

Ashley and her husband, Greg, returned at around five.

As they all stood in the kitchen, Susan and Dennis filled them in on their delightful activities with Leo, barely pausing to catch a breath.

When they did come up for air, Susan noticed Ashley and Greg staring at them with big grins.

She quickly said, "Oh, I'm sorry! We didn't even ask you how your day went."

Ashley shared a coy smile with Greg as she held out an envelope.

"What's this?"

"Open it."

Susan turned to share a puzzled look with Dennis and then opened the envelope to reveal ultrasound photos!

Their jaws dropped.

In unison, Susan and Dennis shouted, "YOU'RE PREGNANT?!"

Ashley nodded excitedly. Then she said,

"Look again!"

Susan and Dennis leaned in and took a closer look. The ultrasound photo was confusing because there were two images.

"It looks like two in there," commented Dennis.

"Yes . . . that's because we're having *identical twins*!"

Little Leo couldn't imagine what had just happened. His parents and grandparents were acting like little kids on the playground . . . jumping up and down and hollering!

The kitchen was filled with shouts of joy and happy tears and hugs all around.

The following week, Susan arrived early for her lunch with Jean. She was so excited she thought she'd burst. Ashley had given her permission to share the big news with her friend and she was rehearsing in her mind how she was going to blurt it out.

Just then the door opened. Jean spotted Susan and made a beeline for her. Susan stood to give her a big hug.

As Jean slipped out of her coat, she read her friend's countenance. "You seem happy!"

"I am! I have something I can't wait to

tell you!"

Jean leaned forward, already smiling at Susan's excitement.

"What is it?!"

"Ashley's pregnant! *With identical twins!* Due in March!"

When the conversation calmed down, Susan told Jean that she and Dennis were thrilled to learn that the twins were girls. "After all, we already have three grandsons: little Leo, plus our son's two boys."

March couldn't come fast enough that year. Susan and Dennis gleefully anticipated their important assignment — watching Leo — while Ashley and Greg were at the hospital for her scheduled C-section.

Around suppertime, Susan and Dennis got the text they were waiting and praying for — "all's well . . . your twin granddaughters, Emma and Sophia, are here!"

They thanked heaven above that their daughter and precious grandbabies were safe and sound. Then Dennis celebrated by marching around the kitchen with little Leo!

Susan thought of family and others who needed to know the good news.

In a bittersweet moment, she wished that she could call her parents — and Dennis's

— to share the incredible joy. But then she smiled, thinking, *They probably already got the news up there and are having a party.*

Oh yes, she remembered, *I have to tell Jean!*

Quickly she texted, "Identical twin girls . . . Emma and Sophia . . . arrived in perfect order!!"

Jean responded immediately.

"Yayy! Congratulations! Let's meet for lunch soon. Send me pictures!"

Before Susan could respond, Jean texted again.

"Could you have imagined that bonus answer on *Wheel of Fortune* tonight?"

Susan was puzzled, wondering, *Why is Jean asking me about* Wheel of Fortune *tonight . . . now . . . when we're elated with our beautiful identical twins?*

She texted back, trying to hide any trace of annoyance.

"No . . . we missed the show. Hearts & minds on news of the twins . . . hands full with Leo! Lol!"

Susan put the phone down.

It dinged again.

"OMG! You missed the Godwink! The bonus answer tonight . . . when the twins were born . . . was IDENTICAL TWINS!"

Susan stared at Jean's message in awe.

She didn't think the day could possibly hold even more joy, but it was a confirmation of God making himself present in this beautiful moment — with an amazing God-wink!

Susan's phone dinged yet again.

Jean was sending a photo she had taken of the television screen with the answer IDENTICAL TWINS spelled out on the big board.

But below the television set at Jean's home, and visible in the picture, was a decorative sign reading "BELIEVE."

Whew! This much joy could tire out a grandmother nutty about grandbabies and *Wheel of Fortune*!

Reflections

Grandparents are beautiful and loving creatures.

Whatever you need, they have it. Lots of it.

You need time? They'll clear their schedule for you.

Advice? Hey, you asked for it!

Unconditional and undying love? You bet. Even more than you can imagine. Forever. And ever.

Watching over, praying for, and guiding our grandkiddies is a joyful gig that never stops.

We may not see it with our own eyes, but their love in return is something we can feel.

I prayed for this child,
and the Lord has granted me what I
asked of Him.
— 1 SAMUEL 1:27 (NIV)

9B
Kirsten — Grandmother's Lost Letter

She must be so disappointed in me, thought Kirsten in a guilt-stricken panic. *Nanny trusted me with that letter and I lost it.*

It was almost too much to bear.

Kirsten Telan, a woman overflowing with effervescent charm and infectious enthusiasm, was normally calm in a crisis. Relying on prayer and common sense to guide her, she strived to find gratitude and a silver lining in all situations.

But that day, Kirsten's inherent optimism failed her.

She had looked everywhere, with still no sign of her beloved grandmother Nanny's letter! It was like it had magically disappeared.

Years earlier, when Kirsten's first child, Kyle, was born, Nanny wrote him a letter, which she presented to Kirsten in a sealed envelope, with instructions to give it to Kyle on his sixteenth birthday. Though that date seemed a lifetime away, Kirsten was determined to follow her grandmother's wishes.

"That's so Nanny," Kirsten told her husband, Pat. "So thoughtful, so loving."

Growing up, Kirsten was exceptionally close to her grandparents, Nanny and Nonno — especially Nanny. If it's true that grandmothers are "a little slice of heaven" in a child's life, Nanny's "slice of heaven" in Kirsten's life was the whole cake!

An Italian immigrant who entered the United States through Ellis Island when she was just seven years old, and then taught herself English, reading, and writing, Nanny was Kirsten's hero. She was always there for her, with unconditional love, a twinkle in her eye, and the best Sunday dinners in the whole wide world.

"She'd begin with a bowl of pasta as an appetizer," Kirsten remembered fondly. Nanny called it "macaroni with sauce," though today it would be known as "penne pasta with marinara." A perfectly cooked roast beef dinner always followed, with broccoli and the creamiest mashed potatoes ever.

The food was always great. But even more, Nanny's dinners were homey.

■ ■ ■ ■

So, for all the above reasons, Kirsten handled Nanny's request about the letter with utmost importance.

Renting a safe-deposit box at her local bank, she carefully placed the letter inside. And for years, that box remained its home.

After a while, Kirsten grew weary of the yearly bank fees and so one day decided to forfeit her safe-deposit box and transfer Nanny's letter to a designated drawer in her desk at home.

Several years and another child later, Kirsten and Pat decided to relocate their family to a new, larger home. They hired a moving company to help them pack up and move.

Somehow, in all the confusion . . . people coming and going . . . Nanny's letter to Kyle completely went out of mind.

Until . . . in a few more years, when Kyle's sixteenth birthday was finally approaching.

Where's Nanny's letter? Kirsten wondered, discovering that it was no longer in the desk.

She couldn't find it anywhere. Upstairs, downstairs, every room in the house . . . she looked in drawers, manila envelopes, photo albums . . . nothing.

Over and over. She scoured the house but found no sign of Nanny's letter.

Where is it? she fretted. *It has to be here somewhere.*

Kirsten was not a person who lost things.

So she prayed. And searched. Then prayed and searched some more. But despite relentless efforts, Nanny's letter remained lost.

Kirsten felt horrible.

"Don't be so hard on yourself," Pat told her one sleepless night. "You know, Nanny would be terribly sad if she knew you were this upset about her letter."

That rang true. Nanny *would* be sad if she knew it was causing Kirsten such distress.

So she stopped. She stopped worrying about the letter. Stopped obsessing over it. And stopped looking for it. But it was never far from her mind.

More years passed. Kirsten's kids graduated from high school and went off to college. Then . . . one day a little fly paid a visit to Kirsten's house.

Now, to say that Kirsten hated bugs would be an understatement.

She had that in common with Nanny,

which is perhaps where she first experienced her creepy feelings about bugs. As a child, Kirsten was amused to watch Nanny scream and chase after a horsefly that had dared to find its way into her home.

So, when a little housefly flew figure-eights through Kirsten's kitchen, you'd think it was the start of World War III.

She swatted and swatted — to no avail.

She looked at the clock; she had errands to run, and it was getting late. So Kirsten paused her war with the fly and went to retrieve her shoes.

But when she reached her bedroom at the back of the house, another fly swooped toward her.

"I cannot believe there are two flies in my house!" Kirsten exclaimed.

Now she was adamant: she would not rest until those flies were gone! The errands could wait another day.

Retrieving a stepstool from the garage, she hauled it back to her closet. There she noticed that *three* flies were now taunting her from a window near the top of the shelf.

She stepped up on the stool — her swatter at the ready — and as she raised her weapon . . . her wrist struck some old photo albums stored on the top shelf.

Down they tumbled, one after another.

In total dismay, Kirsten looked upon the collection of old forgotten albums and photos that had gone askew . . . began to laugh at herself . . . and plopped down in the middle of the mess.

Suddenly a manila envelope floated down — a straggler from the shelf — landing right on Kirsten's head.

"What on earth . . . ?" she sputtered.

She opened the large envelope and her jaw dropped. She was holding Nanny's long-lost letter to Kyle, sealed in a smaller envelope!

Kirsten sat there for ten minutes, crying happy tears . . . laughing with joy.

Looking up, smiling from a tear-stained face, she said, "I know that was you, God! Thank you!"

When Pat came home from work and Kirsten told him what happened, he could hardly believe it.

"Who knew that God would use a posse of pesky houseflies to lead me to Kyle's long-lost letter!"

"What a Godwink," they agreed.

So, at twenty-two years old — six years late — her son finally received his letter from his great-grandmother.

Nanny had written:

> Dearest Kyle . . . how much joy we experienced when you came into our world days ago. How wonderful it was for your grandfather and myself to hold you in our arms. How I wish we could be with you now to see you as a young man.

Nanny went on to write that they had started a fund of two thousand dollars in Kyle's name, maturing at eighteen.

> We want you to always think back to Nanny and Nonno who loved you very very much.

Notwithstanding the sleepless nights endured by Kirsten because of that lost letter, the timing of its discovery turned out to be perfect!

You see, Kyle had become a student at the University of Florida and his grandparents' generous gift came just in time to help him meet his tuition needs.

"God eradicated all my anxiety and replaced it with love, joy, and peace of mind," said Kirsten. "That sounds like God winking to me!"

REFLECTIONS

For everything that is hidden will
eventually be brought into the open,

and every secret will be brought to light.
— MARK 4:22 (NLT)

Have you ever lost something, felt anxious about it, then prayed and found it a short while later?

When something is lost but then is found, there is an array of feelings . . . fear turns to relief, then joy.

Scripture clearly tells us that the Lord cares about all that concerns us. And when you're worrying about a lost item, He wants you to ask for His guidance.

After all, He *is* the world's best tracking device!

Sometimes God will help you find something right away, or, as in Kyle's case, He will wait for the perfect time. Like just when Nanny and Nonno's gift would be even more special and genuinely appreciated.

And we know that in all things God works
for the good of those who love him,
who have been called according to his
purpose.
— ROMANS 8:28 (NIV)

9C
Katie — Grammy Meme's Wedding Ring

Katie never thought one road trip could impact her family so much, but as the car cruised steadily along the highway, no one in the vehicle knew just what was in store for them.

Katie and her husband had joined her widowed father-in-law and his new lady friend, Joyce, on a trip to Myrtle Beach, South Carolina.

It was the first time Katie was meeting her, but she knew this relationship was special. She could tell by the way her father-in-law looked at Joyce.

She carried herself with confidence, had an engaging smile, and wore the most beautiful jewelry Katie had ever seen, especially her rings.

Katie had always loved rings. They reminded her of her grandmother, whom the grandkids called Meme. Many of her rings were given to her by Katie's grandfather, whom everyone knew as Papa.

Yet none was so precious as the one Papa had given Meme on their wedding day.

Katie remembered how Meme's ring looked so regal on her hand. But then, tragically, just after Papa died — leaving Katie's grandmother alone for the first time in thirty-eight years — that magnificent ring was somehow lost!

That's what made it so tragic. Symbolically it seemed as though Meme's grief was doubled.

Everyone in the family pitched in to look for that ring. They searched every inch of Meme's house . . . grilled her on her activities that day . . . what she did . . . where she went.

Meme had run some errands, swung by several stores, and went to watch her grandson's soccer game. When she got home from the game, she noticed the ring was gone.

Meme asked everyone to pray that God would help find the ring. The family formed search teams — even utilizing a metal detector over every inch of that soccer field — but to no avail.

It was lost.

■ ■ ■ ■

"I love your rings," Katie said to Joyce.

Joyce smiled. "Why thank you! You know, every ring has a story."

Katie liked the thought of that.

Joyce took one of the rings off her hand. "Take this one, for example. I came across this ring at work."

Joyce began to explain how she found it just lying on the floor of the pharmacy. She took it to her manager, and they earnestly tried to find its owner.

"For two years!" she emphasized. "My manager posted a sign . . . 'Lost Ring' . . . behind the cashier. All somebody had to do was properly identify it."

She sighed.

"Finally, my manager just gave me the ring and said, 'You take it. I know you'll have a purpose for this ring one day.' "

Joyce passed the ring to Katie. It was stunning, and it really sparkled.

"And you just found it lying on the floor?"

"Right in front of the pharmacy help desk."

Katie thought, *Wow, this really is an incredible story.*

As she turned it in her hand, she was

mesmerized by its sparkle. She almost didn't notice the tiny engraving inside the band. A date . . . that felt familiar.

That's when it hit her. She gasped and grabbed her husband's hand!

"Oh my gosh! This is Meme's ring!" she shouted in excitement.

The date was Meme and Papa's wedding date.

Elated, she began to explain the part of the ring's story that Joyce didn't know. How Katie's grandmother had lost her ring right after her grandfather died.

The family had searched everywhere.

As Katie described Meme, Joyce's face lit up even more.

"I remember her!" she said. "I waited on your grandmother several times when she came into the pharmacy!"

Then, as an afterthought . . . "I wonder why she never checked with us to see if she'd lost it there?"

"Take it . . . please!" Joyce insisted that Katie take the ring and return it to Meme.

The rest of the trip they marveled at how God had written a beautiful new chapter to this ring's story, taking it on a two-year journey . . . divinely aligning Katie and Joyce . . . so that the ring would find its way home.

■ ■ ■ ■

In another perfect alignment, Meme's wedding anniversary was just two weeks away. It was as if God had personally chosen the perfect gift for Katie to give her.

As the family gathered for what would be an unforgettable day, Katie presented a small box to her grandmother.

"What's this?" she asked.

"Open it," Katie replied.

As she lifted the lid, Meme's eyes swelled with tears of joy. She couldn't believe it! The ring that she had lost had finally been found.

There was not a dry eye in the room.

God had given Meme something so special. Not only the ring, but the Godwink connecting her to the love of her life.

Postscript

Sue Wynkoop, Meme's daughter, says that her mother got to enjoy the ring for a couple of years before passing away.

"We always said we'd bury her with that ring," said Sue, "but we didn't . . . she'd taken it off."

During their final conversation, Sue asked

her mother if she wanted to wear her ring. But Meme was insistent: "No, I want you to pass it down!"

So that's what they are doing — using it — and they'll continue to pass it on to the next generation.

"All the children and grandchildren are so excited about it," says Sue. "My sister just wore it to her daughter's wedding . . . and I'll be wearing it to my son's wedding."

Sue loves all the Godwinks that have happened to the family — thanks to that ring — keeping everyone connected to Meme and Papa. She had to tell us one more.

"When SQuire contacted me through Mother's funeral home, they asked, 'Do you know him? Shall I give him your number?'

"After saying 'yes,' I smiled.

"No one had any idea, but SQuire was calling on what would have been mother's ninetieth birthday. Another Godwink!"

Reflections

We often say that a Godwink is a tangible connection to an unseen God. And this time we can almost feel the touch of God's hand in a unique and unexpected manner.

When that amazing Godwink unfolded itself to Katie and Joyce, it gave them reassurance that Our Heavenly Father cares about every detail of their lives.

When Meme was presented with that small ring box, on the very anniversary of her wedding to Papa, we can only imagine the joy that Godwink brought to her — a comforting reaffirmation that God is the finder of all things that are lost.

He will go to great lengths to restore everything from a lost ring to a lost soul.

God, your God, will restore everything
you lost;
he'll have compassion on you;
he'll come back and pick up the pieces.
— DEUTERONOMY 30:3 (MSG)

9D
Grandma Vicki — Best-Timed Godwink Ever

Vicki Chapman loves two things: family and University of Texas football. She was looking forward to both on a Saturday in September.

At her son and daughter-in-law's, it was the usual chaos — yelling and cheering at the TV, eating lots of bad-for-you-but-delicious food, and watching her active — *very active* — grandson Jake run around with endless energy.

"Mimi!" called Jake. "Can you read my book report that's due Monday?"

"Of course, I'd be happy to!"

She read Jake's report and had to admit it was pretty good for a nine-year-old. The book was called *Shoot for the Hoop* and it was easy to see why he would be drawn to it — he loved anything and everything about sports.

The boy in the book was a basketball

player who was diagnosed with a serious illness. His doctor, parents, and coach had to come up with a way for him to continue to play. When he did, he scored the winning point in the game.

Vicki corrected some spelling errors and added a few commas, then told Jake what a great job he'd done.

She was worried about him, though. He was too skinny. She said as much to her daughter-in-law Amy while watching the football game.

"I'm taking him to the doctor on Monday," Amy replied.

In the exam room, Amy could tell that Jake was a little nervous.

"Mom, I don't understand why I'm here."

Amy reassured him that it was just a checkup to make sure that everything was okay.

From the look on the doctor's face, though, everything was not okay.

"I need to tell you somcthing," she said gently. "Jake has type 1 diabetes."

Amy tried to hold it together for Jake . . . but started to cry.

Yet Jake was oddly calm . . . asking a lot of questions. He didn't even seem bothered by having to do finger pricks to test his blood sugar.

"Jake," asked the doctor, "how do you know so much about diabetes?"

"I just did a book report about a basketball player with diabetes," said Jake excitedly.

Amy thought back to the book report her son had just turned in that morning. She vaguely remembered that it was about a boy who got sick. *But diabetes?!*

A few nights earlier, her husband had insisted she make this doctor's appointment because Jake was always thirsty. Then her mother-in-law, Vicki, expressed concern about how thin he was.

Jake was immediately admitted to the hospital.

Amy's number one goal was making sure that Jake knew he could do anything he wanted. That diabetes did not define him.

"Everybody has their something," Amy told Jake warmly. "This just happens to be yours."

Meanwhile, everyone talked about the Godwink, that the very day Jake had been diagnosed with type 1 diabetes (previously known as juvenile diabetes), he had completed a book report on that very topic.

Grandma Vicki reports that of this writing, Jake is twenty-six and doing very well. And guess what? He married a delightful young lady . . . who works in the field of medicine.

That's the way Godwinks unfold. They are little encouragers that work in tandem with other Godwinks to keep on producing signs of hope.

Reflections

Before anyone knew that Jake had diabetes, God knew.

His timing is always perfect.

After reading that book about an athlete who was dealing with exactly the same challenge, Jake was prepared to face the future with confidence knowing that God was already one step ahead of him!

That works for you too.

No matter what difficulty or uncertainty you are facing, trust God — He is always working on your behalf.

Your Father knows what you need before you ask Him.

— Matthew 6:8 (NASB)

10
"Mama Bear" Moms

10A
Eileen —
I'm a "Mama Bear"

Eileen was delightfully married to Jim, a wonderful father to their two children, and who was employed in the auto parts industry. As a public servant in their Pennsylvania community, he volunteered as a first responder on his own time.

Eileen learned that Jim's union was conducting a vote among members to send a small number of representatives to Las Vegas to attend a conference.

"Why don't you put your name in?" she suggested.

Jim's first instinct was that he wasn't qualified. But as Eileen calmly advocated for him to look into it, he became convinced. "Well, why not try!"

Then, when Jim was told he won, that he and his wife were going to Vegas, they jumped for joy, concluding it would be a perfect twenty-fifth wedding anniversary trip!

■ ■ ■ ■

Eileen shared the news with her twenty-two-year-old daughter Kristin, who was working on a new job in Florida for the Orlando Magic professional basketball team. Talk of travel caused Kristin to mention that she had accumulated an impressive number of frequent-flier miles.

"That's great, honey, why don't you join us in Vegas?"

"No, I couldn't do that, Mom. Hey . . . it's your wedding anniversary!"

"Don't give it another thought," said Eileen. "You need a break . . . and it would be fun to have you with us!"

Weeks later the three of them were starting their Vegas adventure with a sightseeing trip to nearby Hoover Dam. It was a hot day, so they welcomed a cool energy drink.

It turned out to be a long day — finally turning in at 11 p.m. Las Vegas time, which was 2 a.m. for their East Coast bodies.

Jim fell asleep first, and in the bed next to them Kristin dropped off for the night.

Eileen couldn't sleep. At 5:30 a.m. she finally started to doze when Kristin's phone rang with a loud and peppy song.

Eileen roused quickly, presuming that one of Kristin's friends in Orlando didn't know she was away . . . or that it was three hours earlier in Las Vegas.

Eileen heard the redundant tune and lyrics sung by Oasis:

. . . after all, you're my wonderwall . . .
maybe
you're gonna be the one that saves me.

Kristin began thrashing! Eileen jumped up, thinking it was a nightmare. But her daughter seemed to be having a seizure and was unconscious!

"Jim . . . wake up! Help Kristin!" she shouted.

Jim immediately began CPR as Eileen ran to the hotel phone. But in the dim light, she couldn't make out the instructions. She shouted to Jim, who left Kristin and dialed the phone, snapping that emergency help was needed as Eileen rushed to the door . . . leaving it ajar!

As Jim resumed CPR, Eileen shouted, "GOD HELP US!"

Instantly a tickling feeling rushed through her body. She was unsure what it meant . . .

but it became evident later that it was the Holy Spirit.

Simultaneously she watched as EMTs on staff at the MGM Grand hotel rushed into the room literally moments after they were summoned . . . and she shuddered as they unpacked paddles to shock her daughter.

One of the EMTs was now ushering her and Jim out of the room.

It must be worse than I imagined, she thought, causing her to pick up the pace on beseeching God, "Please help us!"

Later they learned that it took five shocks. Kristin was breathing again and an ambulance was on the way!

Five days later Kristin was released from the hospital. Jim was unable to attend a single meeting of the conference and almost their entire Las Vegas trip consisted of visits to the hospital.

Kristin returned home with her mom and dad to the suburbs of Philadelphia as Eileen became the family's top detective to determine what in the world happened to her daughter. The hospital's diagnosis that her daughter had a "clinical seizure disorder" didn't feel right.

She began her Mama Bear quest to get solid answers, demanding to know the best doctor in the area. Eileen was pointed to Dr. Sanjay Dixit, head of cardiac electrophysiology at Philadelphia VA Medical Center and professor of medicine at the University of Pennsylvania, who had been recognized for years as one of "America's Top Doctors."

Dr. Dixit's suspicions that Kristin had been misdiagnosed with a seizure disorder were confirmed after he obtained the MGM Grand medical records. It was far more complicated than any of them had imagined.

First, Kristin suffered from long QT, a genetic condition, which they discovered she'd inherited from her father and is described this way by medical authorities:

> Long QT syndrome (LQTS) is a heart rhythm disorder that causes fast, chaotic heartbeats. The irregular heartbeats can be life-threatening. LQTS affects the electrical signals that travel through the heart and cause it to beat.
>
> Long QT syndrome can cause sudden fainting and seizures. Young people with LQTS syndrome have a higher risk of sudden cardiac death.

A heart rhythm disorder that can potentially cause fast, chaotic heartbeats.[3]

It was determined that Kristin had had a heart attack, perhaps made more susceptible by the high-energy drink taken earlier that day, while the jarring sound of her phone in the middle of the night resulted in the long QT triggering her heart to beat improperly. As a precaution, her doctor ordered a defibrillator implant.

By that time, Mama Bear Eileen was counting up the Godwinks, mindful that the EMTs told her they had only seven minutes to stop a heart attack:

What if Eileen had not convinced her daughter to join them on their "twenty-fifth anniversary" celebration in Vegas? She would have been alone in Orlando.

What if they had stayed at a different hotel without EMTs on staff and always on duty, unlike the MGM Grand?

Add to that the Godwinks of discovering lifesaving information about long QT. The family on Jim's side has a history of it,

3 https://www.mayoclinic.org/diseases-conditions/long-qt-syndrome/symptoms-causes/syc-20352518.

including Jim, Kristin, and her first child, Aubrey.

Finally, being divinely aligned with Dr. Dixit was a vital Godwink. His decision to have Kristin's defibrillator implanted paid off quickly. This is how.

Shortly after returning to work, she had a second heart attack, described like being hit in the chest with a baseball. But the defibrillator kicked in, saved her life again, and she's never had a repeat experience.

Mama Bear Eileen will tell you that she has three words to say about taking her daughter to Vegas on their twenty-fifth anniversary: "I love Godwinks!"

Reflections

Godwinks are signs of divine intervention, especially when perceived as the answer to a prayer.

— *When God Winks at You*

When Eileen shouted "God help us!" it was an urgent prayer, directly to heaven, from an overwhelmed and desperate mother.

Right after that she described "a tickling feeling rushing through her body." At the time it was puzzling, but later she concluded it was the Holy Spirit, providing her with assurance that God's angels were on the job . . . and everything was going to be okay.

And it was.

Eileen's supernatural feeling of calmness and peace was also confirmed by the teachings of Jesus:

> But the Counselor, the Holy Spirit, whom the Father will send in my name, will teach you all things and remind you of everything I have told you.
>
> — JOHN 14:26 (CSB)

You can experience the same peace that Eileen felt.

As we say about Godwinks, they are gifts on your doorstep. Just open the door and open your gifts.

The Holy Spirit lives within each of us . . . a gift from God . . . just open your heart and let Him in.

10B
Carla — My Little Girl's Cry in the Night

Carla couldn't wait to fall asleep. Her job had drained every drop of energy these last few weeks.

She crawled into bed, kissed her husband good night, and snuggled into the depths of the down comforter.

Soon she was startled awake. A cry!

She listened.

Was that a cry or was I dreaming?

Then she heard . . . "Mommy!"

Thinking her little four-year-old girl was having a nightmare, Carla jumped out of bed and rushed down the hall to Gabby's room.

In the light from the hall, she could see that Gabby was sitting up and holding her throat. Her eyes were filled with terror and she was struggling to breathe! She made no sound!

"Oh my God, she's choking. Patrick!" Carla screamed to her husband.

Quickly she grabbed Gabby and performed the Heimlich maneuver on her.

One . . . two . . . three . . . and out popped . . . a hard candy!

Gabby coughed and gasped for air . . . her face speaking volumes about the panic she'd just been in.

"Mommy, Mommy . . . you saved me," she said, bursting into tears and throwing her arms around Carla.

"Oh baby, I'm so glad you're okay!"

Carla stroked Gabby's blond shoulder-length hair until her breathing normalized and her little girl eventually fell back to sleep.

Carla didn't realize Patrick was standing right behind her, ready to aid in any way he could.

The moment she saw him she collapsed in his arms, feeling the tension . . . evaporate . . . and whispering in his ear, "Thank you, thank you, God!" She stifled a cry of her own.

Patrick quietly led her from Gabby's room, back to their own bedroom.

"Everything okay now?" he asked softly.

"Yes, thankfully," Carla replied.

"What happened?"

"Gabby was choking on a piece of candy,

but she's fine . . . thank God."

Patrick looked shocked. He had had no idea that such a crisis had just been averted!

After another prayer, they both went to sleep, relieved that their daughter was safe and sound.

The next morning at breakfast, the three of them rehashed what had happened the night before.

"How did you know Gabby was in distress?" Patrick quietly asked Carla.

"She called out 'Mommy!' "

Her husband looked puzzled.

"Honey, I was awake just before you jumped out of bed. Gabby didn't call for you."

"But that's impossible," said Carla, furrowing her brow. "Of course she did, I heard her. Plain as day."

She looked at Patrick with disbelief.

He scrunched up his forehead and shrugged sympathetically.

Rapidly turning to her little girl, she said, "Gabby, you called for me last night, right?"

Gabby shook her head. "No, Mommy . . . I couldn't. I was choking!"

Carla sat back in her chair, stunned. Her eyes filled with tears.

"But . . . I know I heard a voice," she whispered.

Carla and Patrick looked directly into each other's eyes for several seconds, which seemed forever.

They both knew that something supernatural had happened. It was the only explanation.

They simultaneously reached out, held hands, and prayed. As a couple who had been taught the power of partner prayer in a small church group called Couples Who Pray, they had learned to pray together, at least five minutes a day, every day. It was like strapping on the armor of God, without fail.

Carla and Patrick were in the habit of praying together over every issue, big or small.

They had also seen evidence that children who witness their parents praying together, as little Gabby was doing that very moment, will take those value lessons into their own lives, marriages, and families later on.

Gabby slipped in between her mom and dad, adding the perfect punch line to their prayer: "We love you, God!"

REFLECTIONS

We may not always see God but He sees us! He watches over us in more ways than we know . . . when we're asleep and when we're awake.

After that supernatural experience, Carla was filled with a fresh sense of God's amazing love and protection for His children.

There is a beautiful reminder of that in the scriptures:

> Jesus said, "Let the children come to me, and do not prevent them; for the kingdom of heaven belongs to such as these."
>
> — MATTHEW 19:14 (NIV)

Carla followed the Holy Spirit's inner voice that came to her as the voice of her little girl in distress.

May God guide each of us into a fuller understanding of what it means to hear His voice and to listen to where He leads.

> My sheep hear my voice, I know them, and they follow me.
>
> — JOHN 10:27 (CSB)

11
Grieving Moms Find Hope

11A
Mary — Best Mom Ever!

Mary Alexander sat cross-legged on the floor of the closet, lost in sadness.

When she'd gotten up that morning she had the mistaken notion that diving into the drudgery of cleaning out a closet would be a fitting distraction from the sorrow that had again crept over her.

The third Mother's Day was approaching since she had lost her younger son, Jason.

She felt the twinge of disappointment that again she wouldn't be receiving Mother's Day cards from both of her boys this year, as she had enjoyed for so long.

Her other son, Brian, who had lived in Norway for several years, never forgot, and his sweet card had already arrived. She was so appreciative of that.

It was the missing card from the missing son that troubled her.

■ ■ ■ ■

As far back as she could remember, Jason had always made a fuss over Mother's Day. As a child his cards were carefully handcrafted. Then later on, she was told by his friend, he would endlessly search the card shops for one expressing just the right sentiments to touch his mother's heart.

The thought of it filled her eyes with tears. She forced herself to pivot back to the task at hand.

How can you lose a son who's only thirty-nine years old? she asked rhetorically while pulling old papers and magazines from a large cardboard box that had occupied too much space for way too long.

How could the same mother who nursed that child never know that he had an oversized heart? Again she searched her conscience. Should she blame herself? Was there something she could have done to prevent her son's death?

Her urge to cry was momentarily crowded out by a happy thought. Mary fondly pictured Jason that final time he came for Wednesday dinner, which he did every week, almost without fail.

Remembering his boyish blush when she teased him — calling him "her bachelor son," "my six-foot-six gentle giant" or "her baby" — made her smile.

She also loved his sensitivity. Because his older brother could only get back to the States at Christmas, Jason seemed to expand his attentiveness to his mother, as if to help compensate.

Mary remembered Jason's sweet but puzzled countenance that last evening. As he was about to leave she had the urge to hug him extra tight, a little bit longer.

Then, inexplicably, she burst into tears. She quickly chastised herself. After all, she would see him again . . . next Wednesday. *Right.*

That's what she told herself. But her mother's intuition became a tragic reality when she heard the knock on the door at 4 a.m.

She peeked out and saw four police officers standing there. Knowing it couldn't be good news, she screamed for Neil to wake up.

One officer explained that Jason had been to a concert with friends. He told the others he was tired and wasn't feeling well, so someone escorted him to the car to lie down. That's where he was found. A massive heart attack had taken his life.

Only later did an autopsy discover that Jason had an enlarged heart. If he had known about it, perhaps the doctors could have treated him for it.

Sitting on the floor of the closet, replaying the memory of the police speaking in guarded voices, and recalling her sudden sense of collapsing, she again felt tears straining to rise from the back of her throat. She forced her lips tightly together . . . and tried to hold her emotions together.

Frustrated, she roughly shoved the box, but it was too heavy. It didn't budge. She yanked out handfuls of old magazines, slamming them to the floor.

Again reaching into the box, her hand fell upon something. She lifted it up . . . and stopped in her tracks!

It was an unstamped envelope, addressed in a child's handwriting, to the *Potomac News,* which years ago was their local newspaper.

Thirty years had passed since either of her boys had written in that childlike manner.

So whose handwriting is it?

She opened the envelope.

■ ■ ■ ■

It was a newspaper contest, asking for an essay that finishes this statement:

"My mother is the best mom
because . . ."

Now completely dumbfounded, Mary slowly read the child's words:

She's always there when I need her the
most.
Even though I can make her real angry
sometimes,
She always understands because she's
so caring . . .
That's why she'll always be number one
to me.

When she saw the name of the signer, Mary let her tears burst wide-open.

It was Jason Alexander!

In a mixture of melancholy and joy, Mary's tears flowed down her cheeks.

In an instant she realized she was holding a treasured gift that had arrived via special delivery, by the hand of God.

While she was sitting on the floor of her closet, Mary's unspoken prayer was answered — she *would* get Mother's Day cards this year from *both* of her sons: from Jason as well as Brian!

She began dissecting the Godwink. Jason had never mailed his entry to the newspaper, probably for lack of a stamp. But if he had, that little envelope never would have been sitting at the bottom of the box, waiting for his mom to find it, at just the right moment, Mother's Day weekend, thirty years later!

She smiled at the idea that Jason at that very moment was undoubtedly at God's side . . . and both were looking down . . . smiling right along with her!

REFLECTIONS

One of the gifts of motherhood is intuition. Time and time again we have heard about maternal instinct kicking in like protective radar on behalf of children.

Mary felt something was wrong but couldn't pinpoint it. Her extra-tight hug of her son as he left her home was a Holy Spirit nudge that told her that she needed to hold him closer. She had no way of knowing that her time with Jason — in the earthly realm — was coming to a close.

The pain of losing a child that you conceived is simply unthinkable. That's not how it's supposed to be. Mothers are not meant to bury their sons. It is not the natural order of things.

> The Lord is near to the brokenhearted
> and saves the crushed in spirit.
> — PSALM 34:18 (ESV)

That scripture reminds us that at the depths of our pain and sorrow, the Lord is intimately close. He not only understands our brokenness but also has the power to heal the most searing wounds of the heart.

The joyful Godwink of finding a handwritten message from her precious little boy — at the perfect moment — was God's balm to Mary's heart, His comfort to her soul, and a spark to bring a smile to her face.

POSTSCRIPT

Mary had another chapter to this story.

A few years later Mary awoke one morning with another one of those "inspired notions." *Today I'm going to clear out those boxes in the basement!*

Like a rerun from that day in the closet, Mary again struggled with boxes much too heavy for her to move and resolved to simply unpack them, throwing all worthless content into a trash bag.

As she reached down to scoop up the last items at the bottom of one, her hand grasped a chain.

Wait . . . it wasn't just one chain . . . it was two . . . maybe more, all knotted up and wound together!

And something suggested that those were necklaces that Jason had bought on one of his annual cruises.

Mary was reminded that the year before, at a school event, she had lost her favorite necklace, a diamond cross on a silver strand. She told Neil that she didn't want to try to replace it, and not sure why, because she sure missed it.

Returning to the task, Mary sat down, this time pulling up a stool, and meticulously searched for a loose end to one of the silver chains.

Eventually she made progress and concluded that the necklaces indeed belonged to Jason. But then she saw it!

As the second chain unwound, there it was, a little cross. Her heart skipped — a diamond cross on a silver strand!

She looked up and said, “Thank you, God!”

It wasn’t an exact duplicate of her favorite, but somehow . . . it was better.

Once again Mary had been divinely aligned to find a Godwink at the bottom of a cardboard box. Jason was involved in both, and that made this a very special necklace.

She wears it every day.

11B
Laura — Sweet Peacock Godwink

Each of Laura Giffen's three kids was special in their own way, but her daughter Grace had a propensity for flamboyance and attraction.

As an early teen, Laura remembered her daughter as often returning from the store with a bag of glittery things. And it was no surprise that Grace's favorite feathered friend was . . . a peacock!

Images of strutting peacocks adorned her room.

Laura described Grace's memorable attire for her sweet-sixteen birthday party as a peacock-inspired strapless gown with jeweled blue-and-black peacock feathers over the midriff, and black lace flowing from the waist to her ankles. Tilted playfully atop her head, crowning her pulled-back, gleaming brown hair, was a dapper little top hat, blue and black, that continued the dress's jeweled theme. Grace's poise and beauty were that of a cheeky *Cosmopolitan* model.

The delightful photos from the party showed Grace as a confident, smart-looking young woman who had the world at her fingertips.

Sadly, outside of her immediate family and close counselors, people may never have imagined that Grace was hiding something: an insidious mental health condition that resulted in extreme changes in her mood, leaving her depressed and distant.

In a moment, Grace's joyous, exuberant nature could plunge into sadness. Despite an abundance of compassionate family and friends who deeply loved her, Grace descended into a dark abyss of depression.

That depression caused her to lose hope and eventually . . . the will to live.

That tragic day will never be erased from the memory of Laura and her husband . . . the day they discovered that their precious little girl had taken her own life.

Every parent who tragically walks upon that same horrible path will ask a thousand times, "Why? What could I have done? When will the pain go away, God?"

"We struggle with it every day," says Laura. "We realize that we're never going to have all the answers. . . . That's why we've learned to rely on our faith."

Laura asked God to send a sign — "a really big sign" — to let her know that her daughter was okay, and up there with God in heaven.

Then she got the sign.

One January morning she and her husband looked out on the deck and there walking around . . . was a peacock!

What in the world? They'd never seen a peacock in their rural area!

Laura knew right away that this must have been a Godwink straight from above.

She immediately did the motherly thing: she fed their new friend and gave her a name, Sweet Pea. In the beginning, she assumed the peahen was just stopping off on its journey to someplace. But after several months they came to the conclusion that they *were* the place!

About the time that Laura was approaching that difficult day — the anniversary of the loss of Grace, on the eighth of April — she decided to reach out to Jeanne, her former coworker whom she heard was not doing well, suffering from ALS, a debilitating disease.

She fondly recalled how Jeanne was her

best workplace ally after Grace died. To cope with her grief, Laura had taken several weeks off and Jeanne kept in touch, all along.

When Laura was to return to work, she dreaded that many well-meaning colleagues might be asking redundant questions too painful to answer.

It was Jeanne who volunteered to handle everything and for days served as an angelic bodyguard, at Laura's side from the parking lot to her desk, helping her transition back into the routine.

Now it was Laura's opportunity to return the favor, to help Jeanne cope during her last months of life.

Unable to speak verbally, Jeanne was able to text. So Laura would tell Jeanne stories about the adventures of Sweet Pea that day, which became a pretext for talking about her dear daughter Grace. For instance, she texted pictures of the peacock in juxtaposition with photos of Grace in her peacock gown at her sweet sixteen.

Nonverbally they spoke about death, God, and heaven. And Jeanne shared that she was growing less anxious and more accepting about transitioning to her heavenly home.

Jeanne suggested that Laura write a children's book about the amazing Godwink of Grace and Sweet Pea, and encouraged Laura to get started on that project.

One day Laura received a note from Jeanne's husband. Her friend had graduated to heaven.

"Together we found faith and hope in our grief," said Laura. "Our coming together was divinely aligned . . . and so was Sweet Pea's arrival."

That was confirmed a day or two later. Sweet Pea disappeared . . . leaving behind a feather . . . Her job was finished.

REFLECTIONS

The peacock is one of God's most magnificent creatures. Their iridescent colors are one of the beauties of nature. And the way they walk with a strut seems to emphasize their endearing flamboyance and demand for attention . . . just like Grace, who must have enjoyed being the photo op of the sweet-sixteen party.

When we stop to think of it, God often uses birds to send Godwinks of assurance, letting each of us know He is never apart from us.

When Sweet Pea disappeared, theatrically leaving behind a single feather, God was signaling that her job was finished. It sent a clear message to Grace's parents that their beautiful daughter was free as a bird from the torments of earth, and enjoying all of heaven's colors . . . said to be more plentiful and beautiful than we could ever imagine.

Laura says in a note to us, "I wanted to share this Godwink story in the hopes it would provide hope and peace to others."

She also observed: "Isn't it amazing how our God finds ways to build us up, while engaging us in work to encourage others? And invariably his Godwink gifts to us are more touching when shared with someone who can benefit."

Today, look for your Godwinks; appreciate that they have been sent to you by "special delivery" to provide hope and peace.

> A generous person will be enriched, and the one who gives a drink of water will receive water.
>
> — PROVERBS 11:25 (CSB)

Thank you for joining us on this journey of how God's grace and Godwinks are sprinkled into the lives of mothers . . . the dearest souls of nearly every family on earth.

We pray that you were touched by these

true stories. Perhaps even encouraged or inspired. And we'd love to hear from you: www.Stories@Godwinks.com.

— SQuire and Louise (aka SQuise)

ACKNOWLEDGMENTS

Godwinks for Moms is our thirteenth Godwink book — our seventh in the Simon & Schuster/Atria Godwink series — and one of our favorites under the extraordinary leadership of Peter Borland, vice president and editor-in-chief of Atria Books.

For the Godwink book series, we are grateful for the kind and brilliant guidance of Jennifer Gates, our outstanding literary agent.

We express heartfelt thanks to each person who shared their Godwink story in this book, recognizing that all of these chronicles are personal family treasures.

For *Godwinks for Moms* we were fortunate to assemble a terrific research team to assist with initial interviews on the stories and contribute to shaping the outcome. We are very appreciative for the talents of Judith Lawson, Kathryn Dow, Robin Taney, Anthony Knighton, and our team coordinator,

Hilary Kitzman.

Thank you, all!

SQuire and Louise

ABOUT THE AUTHOR

Godwinks for Moms is the seventh book coauthored by **SQuire Rushnell** and **Louise DuArt.** SQuire is a popular speaker, Emmy Award winner, and *New York Times* bestselling author who has coined the term "Godwink," now in mainstream usage. With more than two million books in print, he's executive produced four Hallmark Godwink Movies which have premiered #1, while Netflix's Godwink Brand movie *Rescued by Ruby* has had over 100 million views in its first year. His Godwink stories have been a popular monthly feature for many seasons on *Today* and he's a familiar face on CBS *Sunday Morning,* Fox New Channel's *Fox & Friends,* CBN's *The 700 Club,* TBN's *Huckabee,* and many others. As a veteran ABC Television Network executive, he led *Good Morning America* to the number one spot and is one of the fathers of the acclaimed

Schoolhouse Rock series and ABC *Afterschool Specials.* Louise is a touring Women of Faith speaker who has hosted a popular daily talk show, *Living the Life,* on ABC Family, and has starred in various Broadway productions. One of the world's top comedic impressionists, Louise has starred in sold-out performances for fifteen years. Clean and funny, she executes fast-paced conversations between herself and Bart Simpson, Judge Judy, Barbra Streisand, Hillary Clinton, and dozens more. Together, SQuire and Louise are the founders of Pray Together Stay Together, a nonprofit that advocates healing relationships by praying together five minutes a day for forty days. They live on Martha's Vineyard.

www.ingramcontent.com/pod-product-compliance
Lightning Source LLC
Jackson TN
JSHW082323280825
90082JS00002B/2
* 9 7 8 1 4 2 0 5 2 7 5 8 2 *